To Hell

Journaling Your Way to a New Normal

Judy Keith, Ed.D

Table of Contents

Dedication

This book is dedicated to my husband, Leonard Joe Keith, and our sons, William Ross Keith and Christopher Michael Keith.

Acknowledgments

I am grateful to Liz Habermann for her friendship and insights into how to organize this book. I am also grateful to the following friends: Donna Vandy, retired school counselor; Delores Allen Carpenter, retired social services worker; Chris Froehlich, long-time friend; and my son Christopher Michael Keith for their suggestions.

About the Author

Dr. Judy Keith grew up in a large family in southwestern Virginia. She completed an undergraduate, master's, and doctoral degree before becoming a university professor in health education. After her husband and son's deaths, she became a nationally recognized consultant training school staff to work with students who had experienced a death or trauma. This heartfelt book, To Hell and Back is her description of her own recovery from losses and includes a chapter to aid the reader in journaling their personal losses.

Chapter One: Introduction

This is the story of the loss of my husband at age thirty-one, my son at seventeen, and how I grieved issues from my childhood. An additional chapter includes journal entries for you to use in processing and recording your life and loss experiences. Writing and drawing are techniques helpful in understanding and releasing emotional and mental pain and are evidence-based strategies for reducing stress. While some people find it difficult to start writing, once you do, you will find using a journal extremely helpful throughout life.

There is no right or wrong way to feel when a loss occurs. All feelings are normal. Recovery is a unique process for you and for the relationship shared with the person who died. How, when, and with whom you share these feelings is sometimes difficult to judge but is a choice only you can make. Not all people you know will be comfortable with your pain. If not, they probably have not yet had a significant loss, so they may not understand how to be helpful or supportive. When there is no one around to talk with, use the time to write or draw in your journal. I suggest you use your computer or a separate unlined journal for writing and drawing purposes.

You may want to date each entry so you can read through your entries later. Sometimes reviewing over time what you have written brings to mind other issues, and you will decide to write more when you reread your writing. You will gain many insights into your life as you work through your grief. Grieving is work! Dr. William Worden, a noted grief researcher, and therapist, suggests you must address the following Tasks of Mourning to complete your grief work. The first task is to accept that the person is dead. For some, not having the body or not being able to view the body makes this task difficult. Because of the impact of shock, you may participate in closing rituals but still not fully accept that the person is dead.

The second task of mourning is to review your life experiences with the deceased and process any unfinished issues that may have occurred. This task is not difficult if you have a loving relationship free of conflict with the deceased. The unfinished business that did conflict may require letter writing to confront or apologize to the deceased. The third task of mourning requires that you adjust the roles and responsibilities fulfilled by the deceased by either reassigning them to another family member, assuming them yourself or learning to live without them. The final task of mourning is to renew life by reinvesting in living and establishing a new normal. The grief process for an adult who is expecting the death to occur takes about two and a half years to complete. The process could take longer if the death was sudden and involved trauma such as an accident, murder, suicide, dismemberment, or abuse. If the person who died is your child, the grief process can take six to eight years to complete. It is important to note that culturally people give the grieving person until the first anniversary of the death to finish their grief work and may begin to pressure them to 'get on with life' too soon. The concept of 'closure' is another area of misconception. There is no true end to the grief process, as many assume. Because love is the bond to the deceased, and love never ends, you may be triggered throughout your life by thoughts or reminders of the deceased. The pain is usually less intense later in life, and you experience this reaction less frequently as time passes. This, too, is normal. Time does not heal, but processing your thoughts and feelings regarding memories of your relationship with the deceased does lead to healing. If you do not face the pain, learn the life lessons and grow from them, you may become stuck in a less fulfilling life than you deserve.

After my son's death, as I was considering leaving the university to become an independent consultant, I was thinking about what to call my consulting company. I had completed a substantial amount of grief work for my husband but not for my son. I was driving through Fort Payne, Alabama, when the name was given to me. I have often felt that insights have come through me and not from me. I was thinking about the grief process and what I would hope others could come to understand through my work. The goal of grief work is to complete the tasks of mourning so you can RENEW life again. The symbol of this new life or rebirth for me became the butterfly. Reading and journaling taught me that the Center for Personal Recovery is within each of us. We may feel that our heart is broken or there's a hole in our hearts, and grief work is the CPR treatment. The rose represents the love that never dies, and the butterfly represents rebirth or the beginning of a new life after a death occurs. The use of a journal to process your life experiences is an evidence-based tool that can reduce your stress and help you identify life lessons unique to you. Take time to heal. Be gentle with yourself but make working through your grief a daily practice. Know that you can experience peace and find joy in life again. I have chosen to share some of my journey through grief to encourage you to embark on yours. Judy Keith, Ed.D.

Chapter Two: The Loss of a Husband

Early losses we experience as children can impact how we grieve significant losses later in life. Until Joe's death, I had little experience with death. My maternal grandmother, Viola, died of breast cancer when I was in third grade. I remember only that my mother was sad and tearful and I got a new dress and black patent leather shoes to wear to the funeral. Growing up, I remember seeing pictures of Viola in her casket but have no memory of the funeral itself. Mom had also been depressed after she lost a baby between me and my brother Charles.

The wakes and funerals I attended as a child were scary to me because we were not told what to expect to see and hear. The preaching was more about saving souls than celebrating the life of the deceased. As a child, I had formed no opinion about what happened after death. It was only later in life that I realized Joe's body had died, but his soul had transitioned to another place.

Death was actually a very scary thing for me as a child. I grew up in the mountains of Southwestern Virginia, where hard-shell Baptist churches were common. Wakes and funerals were frequently held in family living rooms. The preaching was nonsensical to me because the preachers yelled, held their ears for some strange reason as if they were listening to God, said, "Ah" as they gasped for breath, and blew their noses frequently. Their messages were about sin and burning in hell if you were not saved and baptized. Baptism was done in the local river near the low water bridge. Singing on those occasions was by line, meaning someone would say a line, and then everyone would join in by singing the line. The thought of God being a loving, caring, and forgiving entity was not preached.

When a death occurred, our mother cooked food to take to the family, and flowers were sent. Adults often sat for a time at the wake. The women would sit inside the house while the men stood outside and smoked. Most of the time, several preachers spoke and there was the singing of hymns. The same service was held at the funeral; women often cried hysterically, and some passed out.

Because there were so many of us (seven siblings), our financial resources went to food, clothes, gas for daddy to get to work, and medicine when we were sick. Pets were not common but I was allowed to have a kitten when I was young. I named him Ricky after the popular singer Ricky Nelson. Ricky developed a boil on his side and died. I had to bury him and went there daily to cry.

I met my future husband in college during a failed attempt to complete a woodworking project in the evening woodworking class called Westervelt. Someone else was using the tool I needed, and I was standing there frustrated. Joe Keith, an industrial art major, started a conversation with me, and I immediately realized he was a caring person and a good listener. He asked me out, and our lives together began at that moment.

Joe was born in Eastern Kentucky in a community called Leatherwood. His father was a journeyman carpenter. Joe had two brothers, and he was the youngest son. His brothers came to Berea, Kentucky, to attend the Foundation High School at Berea College. When Joe came to attend Berea Foundation, his parents moved to Berea too. His mother took a job working in a factory. All three brothers served in the military during the war in Vietnam. Joe was in the Seabees unit of the navy while his brothers served in the army. I met Joe after his military experience when he returned to college.

Joe was the love of my life. Marriage was inevitable. Because we were students at a work-study college, we were responsible for supporting ourselves. I made my wedding dress, and the wedding was simple. Since my dad didn't like to travel, my younger brother Charles walked me down the aisle of the Catholic Church because Joe was Catholic. We lived on a shoestring budget, but I cannot remember a happier time in my life. Our first son was born. Billy was tiny because of the genes passed from my maternal grandparents, and he was a little early due to my having the flu. My sister Nina came to stay with us for a week until I was well enough to care for him. I was afraid to bathe him at first, so I gave him his bath in a white plastic mixing bowl. Joe was going to school and working. He did night duty with the baby until I was well enough to do so. One day he came home for lunch and made me soup. I was so weak I couldn't feed myself. He fed me. I can't remember my mother even doing that for me when I was sick. Billy was so cute and the sweetest baby. He was also the Keith family's first grandchild, so he was well loved. Joe and I could not have been prouder of our first son. Joe loved to put him in a backpack and ride him around campus on his bicycle. As Billy grew, he graduated to a baby seat attached to the bike.

Joe was loving, affectionate, thoughtful, kind, and generous. In addition to our family, he was always doing things for his parents, my parents, and friends. He was respectful and hardworking and put family first.

Joe's first job out of college was as an admission counselor for Berea College, which required extensive traveling in the Appalachian states. I lived in fear of him being killed in a car accident. It seemed I had a premonition. So, I nagged him into applying for a head resident's position for a men's dorm at Eastern Kentucky University. When he took this job, it allowed him to be home every day, and my anxiety diminished. He wanted desperately to have a daughter, so we read a book about determining the sex of your baby, charted my periods, and got pregnant. I lost the baby before three months. My mother called me the day I miscarried because she felt something was wrong. We tried to get pregnant again as soon as we could, but Chris, our second son, didn't come along until Billy was five. Joe attended childbirth classes with me and was present during Chris' delivery. Again, Joe floated in the air with pride. Billy loved his baby brother, but as they grew up, the age difference sometimes led him to consider Chris a pest. Once Billy emptied the toy box, helped Chris inside, and sat on the lid.

Since Joe and his dad were both carpenters, they planned to build our first home. We purchased five acres of land outside Berea and selected a house plan. Joe loved to go to the mountain and think about what he had to do. His college professor from whom we purchased the land suggested that he needed to use a tractor to pull up the small trees so he could dig the footer for the foundation without having to dig up the tree roots. I objected and offered to buy him a chain saw. The last conversation we had was as near to an argument as we ever had. He told me he knew what he was doing, and the roots had to be pulled first. He needed a chain to put around the trees, so he went to his dad's that Saturday morning, November 13, 1977, to borrow one. His dad also tried to convince him not to use the tractor, but he still gave him the chain. Joe left in a huff. He hooked the chain to the front implement hook on the tractor instead of to the wheelbase, which caused an imbalance in the tractor. He died instantly when the tractor flipped the first time he tried using it to pull a small tree.

The journey through grief is an experience unique to the individual and to the life events shared with the deceased. My grief journey began when I received the bad news.

I cleaned house as I always did on Saturday morning until my anxiety could no longer be contained. I called his dad and told him I was worried because Joe had not come home. His dad and the college professor who had sold us the land and loaned him the tractor went to the mountain and found him. His neck and back were broken, and his lower jaw and skull were crushed. Nearly panicked, I paced the floor until I got a call from his mother. She said, "Little boy is gone."

I said, "Gone where, Mother? He would never leave without telling me where he was going."

She said, "Little boy is dead."

I said, "No, Mother."

I grabbed the kids who were in their pajamas and drove like a bat out of hell to his parent's house. I knew immediately there was something wrong when I arrived because the lights were on and the door was wide open. I ran throughout the house looking for them. I learned later that as soon as Mom got off the phone with me, she and Dad had driven to my house. After finding no one at home, I drove to the mountain. I remember speeding through the small town of Berea. Billy was holding Chris in the front seat, singing him nursery rhymes, but Chris would not stop crying. When we arrived at the farmhouse at the base of the mountain, cars were parked all over the yard, and an ambulance was trying to get up the old farm road to the mountain top. I remember thinking that was strange and wondering why all those cars were there surrounding a house at the bottom of the mountain. My sister-in-law and brother-in-law met me in my car.

Lee said, "Judy, you need to stay down here. He's hurt really bad, but he is not dead."

I passed out. When I regained consciousness, I was lying on the farmer's bed, surrounded by strangers. My sister-in-law, Joan, had taken the boys to her mother's house. I got up and started running toward the mountain with Lee chasing me, telling me not to go up there. I screamed at him, "I can help him stay alive."

When I got to the top of the first hill, the college professor and a state trooper met me. The trooper asked if I was Mrs. Keith, and I said yes. He said, "I'm sorry, but your husband is dead, and you don't need to see him. You need to go back to the farmhouse."

When I turned around, Lee was standing behind me. I started hitting him with my fists. I screamed, "You lied to me!" In the process of hitting him, I knocked my own glasses off and broke them. Lee drove me to his mother-in-law's house. I took the boys into the bathroom for privacy, put both of them in my lap, and told them daddy's body was dead, and dead meant that daddy was never coming home again. Billy, at seven years old, could understand what I said, but Chris, at two years old, could not comprehend. He would tell people his daddy was dead and then ask me when he was coming home. I didn't know until much later that my boys' reactions were normal for their developmental levels.

I remember nothing after that encounter until the next morning. I was lying on Mom and Dad's sofa when the front door opened, and two of our friends, Chuck and Liz, burst through the front door with panic on their faces. They had heard the news on the radio.

I remember nothing else until someone had to go to the funeral home to view the body and decide to have an open casket. Joe's dad was under the care of his doctor then. The task fell to me. My youngest brother, Ike, accompanied me. The funeral director walked me near the casket and told me he had done the best he could. The face I saw looked like a strange man with large jaws. His hair was down in his face, nearly covering his eyelids, so I reached down to comb it back with my fingers. I glanced at his hands to see if his wedding band was still there. It was, but I also saw dirt under a fingernail. Joe always cleaned his nails after working on the mountain. I passed out but always regretted not asking the funeral director to clean his nails better. The casket was closed. Mama Keith never saw the body and later asked me if it was really Joe in the casket. Billy asked me once if I was sure his daddy was dead and if I was sure his daddy was in the casket. I assured him he was dead and inside the casket. He asked me if his daddy was smiling, and I told him yes, which was a lie, but he wanted to know if his daddy was happy in heaven.

So, when the time came for Joe's funeral, I was filled with dread. I made myself dress. Joe loved to buy me clothes, so I picked a pale blue sheath he had given me. As I was dressing, my pantyhose developed a runner, so I went to the local drugstore to buy a new pair. Joe hated to see my slip hanging or a runner in my hose. The sales lady seemed very uncomfortable serving me but allowed me to use the employee's bathroom to change my hose. I didn't understand her reaction to me. I assumed she thought I was prideful about my appearance on the day of my husband's funeral while I was merely honoring him. At the funeral, I remember only the priest who married us, speaking along with a minister I didn't know from the university. Everything else about the funeral was not stored in my memory.

My mother stayed with us for a week, and I'm sure she took good care of the boys, although that, too, was lost to the blackness that enveloped me. She had to go home, and I had to get myself together for the boys' sake, but I don't remember what I did. I had trouble believing he was really dead and felt like I was stuck in a nightmare. As if operating on a remote control, I picked up the phone two weeks after Joe's death and called his office. When his secretary, Kathy, answered, I realized I was trying to call a dead man. I hung up the phone without speaking.

Joe died on November 13, 1977. The holidays were coming up for the family, and I was not functioning. During Christmas and Thanksgiving holidays, we usually went to Joe's parents' house for a meal, but a couple of our friends offered to help me with Thanksgiving dinner at my house. Mom, Dad, and a couple of friends came, but all other details were lost to the darkness. My only memory of our first Christmas without Joe had to do with the Christmas tree. Joe made Christmas so much fun. He dressed as Santa and came out of his parents' attic with a sack of toys for the grandkids. That image was the only memory of his dad that Chris had. Joe always cut a real tree for his parents and us. The first Christmas without him, I couldn't bring myself to get a tree. I kept thinking about what Joe did and how whatever I did would be inadequate. The previous year Joe had asked a farmer if he could cut a tree on his land, then taken both boys to get the preselected tree, put it in the stand, and put the lights on it. The boys and I finished decorating it. For the dorm, he and several students took a truck and trailer to get a tree that was two stories high. How could I top that? On Christmas Eve, I picked up a dead tree from the temporary lot along the roadside and struggled to get it into the stand.

The end of the tree was uneven, so in retrospect, I should have found the handsaw and cut it off straight, but I didn't have the energy. I leaned it up in the corner of the room and put on the electric lights. The tree fell over, and half the lights quit working, so I bought more at a drugstore.

By the time I actually got it ready for the boys to decorate, it was past their bedtime, and we were all grumpy. The second year I bought a live tree which nearly gave me a hernia dragging it into and out of the house. It died soon after it was planted in the backyard. The next year I bought a Norfolk pine which looked weird according to them. The following year we decorated a fig tree. The fifth year I bought an artificial tree. What an insult to the boys, and they let me know it. I couldn't satisfy them. I tried to distract them from the tree by giving them a new ornament each year and making them identical stockings.

At the time of Joe's death, we rented an old university house, and since my husband no longer worked for the university, the boys and I had to move. His father found me a house in Berea, so I bought the small three-bedroom, bath-and-a-half house with a big backyard. His parents kept the boys until our furniture was moved to the new house. The night before the move was scheduled, it snowed 13 inches, but the movers said they could do it. Everything was loaded, but the moving van was stuck in the yard. A wrecker was called to free the truck. Before we made it to the new house, the truck slid into a ditch, and another wrecker had to be called. By the time we finally arrived at the house, everyone's nerves were on edge. Two of the movers got into a fight in the back of the truck and refused to move anything else. I trudged out to the truck and told them they either moved our things into the houses or they would not get paid a dime! They finished the move. By then, it was dark, so I stayed in the empty house surrounded by boxes. The boys stayed with Mom and Dad. I was exhausted and went to bed, fully dressed. I had my first nightmare that night about Joe being killed and woke in a full-blown panic attack. I had no idea what was happening to me. Frightened, I began frantically pacing the house. Gradually I calmed down, but my mind still raced with crazy thoughts. I was losing touch with reality, so I looked for something to use for writing. I found a roll of paper towels and a blue felt tip pin I had used to label the moving boxes. My thoughts flowed onto the paper until I was exhausted. I fell asleep on the unmade bed with my clothes on.

Months went by with me mechanically taking care of the boys, getting Billy to school, and existing. I have little memory now of any of that time. Someone encouraged me to see a doctor, so I made an appointment. He did not tell me that I was depressed. I suppose a 30-year-old is not expected to be depressed, but looking back, I understand now that I had clinical depression. Instead of anti-depressant medication, he offered me Valium to take as needed for the panic attacks. I refused. Good thing I refused because, in my state of mind, I would have become addicted.

Questions haunted me in an endless cycle. 'If only' I had nagged him to stay home that day? 'Why me?' 'Why him?' 'What had I done to bring this disaster into our lives?' I found no acceptable answers because all I wanted was him back alive with us.

Billy struggled with these questions too. He would say, "If I had been there, I could have gotten that tractor off him." So, I took him to see the tractor and let him try to lift it. Then he said, "If I had been there, I could have run for help and saved him." I told him his dad died instantly and no one could have saved him. His final comment was, "If I had been there, I could have died too."

My response was, "Oh no. Mommy couldn't live without you, and daddy would not have wanted that to happen."

I had a job as executive director of a public health agency at the time of Joe's death. Although the boys were getting social security benefits, I still needed to work. Going back to work the first day was really hard. I drove Billy to the front of the school and let him get out to go into the school alone. Overwhelmed myself, I had no idea if an adult greeted him or helped him make the transition back to school. After getting Billy to school and Chris to the babysitter, my routine was to have coffee at the drug store near my office. On my first day back to work, I remember walking into the drugstore through the back door. The same people I had coffee with every morning were all sitting around the counter. When they saw me, they stopped talking and looked at the counter. Only one stool was left, so I took it. The waitress put my coffee in front of me without a word. The silence was so strange. There was no discussion of basketball, farming, politics, or the weather…just dead silence. I realized that the problem was me. I made them uncomfortable. I ran to my office and never drank coffee there again. My staff was very understanding and covered for me as best they could. I had no memory. I could not think and plan as I had before. I realized that I was not doing my job well enough to earn my salary, so I gave the board my resignation.

I decided to stay home till I was able to function. I didn't shower for days and wore the same clothes repeatedly. I didn't get a haircut, ate very little, and lost more weight.

After the boys were asleep, it was always my time to cry. Sometimes during the day, I would go to the cemetery, lay on the ground, beat my fists on his grave, and cry. When all my feelings were released, I would pick up the kids, gather some flowers, and take them to the cemetery. One day Billy asked me, "Mommy, why don't you cry? Don't you miss my daddy?" I knew instinctively that I was doing the boys a disservice by hiding my grief. I decided to cry in front of them and to talk about Joe more.

Billy loved Saturday morning cartoons. One morning Chris, age two and a half, pulled the knob off the tv, and I could not replace it. In frustration, Billy said, "Mommy, I can't live without a daddy. Are you ever going to marry again?"

I said, "Well, finding someone to marry is not easy, and your daddy was special. Think about all the people we know. They are all married. I don't know anyone who isn't married. Do you?" Thinking I had answered his question, I went back to house cleaning.

Shortly afterward, he bounced into the room with a big smile on his face. "I've got it, Mom. We can run an ad in the newspaper. Father needed. Two fine sons." My heart could not consider remarriage, although his parents had told me it was okay because they thought the boys needed a father.

Remarriage and dating seemed to be a theme for friends and even strangers.

One day a woman I knew only by name stopped me on the street during my many walks to ask when it was appropriate to remove her wedding ring. I asked her why she thought I would know. She replied, "Well, you've been widowed longer than me, and someone has asked me out. I feel uncomfortable wearing my wedding ring." My hand was covering my rings. I went home and thought about that encounter. I took my rings off and felt naked. I put them back on and realized I needed to do something. Finally, I decided to have a jeweler make my wedding band into a pinkie ring which I wear to this day. My engagement ring was later used initially by Chris to ask his wife, Lynette, to marry him. They returned the ring with the diamond made into a drop necklace after he bought her a ring. On another walk, an older woman stopped me to lament that it was easier for me to be a widow at a younger age. I could not understand her view. I would love to have had forty years with Joe instead of a little over eight.

A year later, I made friends with a man interested in buying Joe's van. We talked almost every night by phone. Nights were my worst time because that had been mine and Joe's personal time. The friend's name was Joe also, and he listened well. One morning two years later, I was having a cup of hot tea on the patio. The fog was coming over the mountains behind the house. The birds were singing, and daffodils were blooming by the steps. For so long, my world had been colorless and all my senses dulled by pain. The breeze was refreshing. I looked at the pottery mug I had bought from my friend and realized I had made one new friend. I also realized that another friend had always given me tea when I visited her, and I now liked the taste. I could see the flowers and hear the birds. I vowed to learn to live again!

Joe and I had started a small craft store in Berea, so when I quit my professional job, and Chris stayed with me after school while I worked there. One day an older college student stopped to talk with Chris and Billy. He was divorced and missed his son. My boys were thrilled with his attention, so he stopped by the store frequently. Billy invited him to his t-ball game, and he invited us to his dorm's open house. On the day of the open house, I received red roses with no name on the card. When we visited him in the dorm, he gave me the 12th rose. He came to the t-ball game and sat with us. My brother-in-law was not happy! He came to see me the next day to tell me he was upset. I told him the man was just a friend. His response was he would never be okay with me seeing another man, friend, or otherwise. He lived up to that comment. Even in church all these years later, he refuses to speak to me. His wife, Joan, does.

My first real date was arranged by a friend who pressured me to have dinner with one of her friends. He was a college professor, never married, and had a good reputation. Finally, I caved in and agreed. I hired a babysitter to stay with the boys. He cooked a gourmet meal and tried his best to keep me engaged in conversation. I felt like I was betraying Joe and still felt married. The babysitter asked me how the date went, and I swore never to go out with anyone again. Later that same year, my dentist asked me to come to his and his wife's Derby party. I wasn't much of a party goer, but friends encouraged me to go. I asked my new telephone friend, Joe, to go with me. He refused, saying I just wanted him to keep the men away. I never thought of that because my issue was anxiety and social awkwardness. I went alone and what a mistake that was! Every single man and some married men tried to talk to me, with one continually invading my personal space. I left the party before the Debry race and called Joe as soon as I got home. He said, Judy, they see you as single, and you see yourself as married still. How astute that observation was.

During my lost period, I had no strengths, only weaknesses. There were days I just knew I was going crazy. My thoughts were out of my control, and my emotions, likewise. The first source of outside information was a book given to me by another widow. The title is *How to Survive the Loss of a Love* by Melba Colgrove. Then another friend gave me *Widow* by Lynne Caine. From there, I read anything I could find that might help me understand what I was going through. I was so lost that I was unaware that Billy was struggling in school. One night his teacher called. She was a widow, too, but her children were older. She told me Billy was struggling and could not keep a pencil; if he finished his homework, lost it, or forgot to turn it in, I needed help. I discussed her call with a friend who recommended a good counselor for children. Billy never went to the male counselor, but the man listened well to me and gave me mostly good advice on how to help the boys. The biggest mistake he made was to advise me to keep putting Chris back in his big boy bed when he crawled into bed with me at night and just let him cry himself to sleep. I REALLY regret following his advice. I should have comforted him more.

I missed talking with Joe so much. Every worry, every task that had to be done would have been easier if only I could talk them through with him. But most of all, I wanted one more chance to tell him how much I loved him. If I had one more opportunity to talk with him, I would say, "I will always love you. Thank you for the happiest years of my life." The thing I missed most was having someone special to love me. Loneliness to me was feeling like no one else cared. The thing I enjoyed most was the time we spent together as a family; now, our family felt incomplete.

My eating habits changed, and food was not a necessity. I was a size three when Joe and I married. Baby weight gain was lost quickly after each pregnancy, so when he died, I had little weight to spare. I looked emaciated two years after Joe's death. I was a terrible cook, and the food had no taste. I could go days without eating, but I prepared food for the boys anyway.

I never felt so alone in my life. Nights were the worst because sleep seemed an illusion, and the nightmare came back when I did dream. One night I woke from that dream and looked around the new bedroom filled with our furniture, and the realization that he was dead hit me hard. I had a panic attack, so I walked about the house for hours. The next day I told my friend, Liz, what had happened. She told me I didn't have to go through that kind of experience alone. I could call her anytime, night or day. She is still my friend 45+ years later. Sleep patterns can change when you are grieving; your doctor should be informed. I never went back to a doctor for fear drugs would be pushed on me.

I found some female friends uncomfortable with me, and I didn't understand why. I was a fifth wheel in a couple's world. A few dropped out of my life when I started trying to put my life back together. Sometimes, people said what my son Chris called 'dumb and stupid things'. These people used clichés when they did not know what to say. These clichés were irritating and hurtful.

When someone says, "I know how you feel," they are thinking about their own loss. When they say, "God doesn't give you more than you can handle," "God has a purpose," and "It was his time," they are trying to give you their beliefs taught in church. Those comments did not make me feel any closer to God. If you have faith, you don't need theirs. If you don't have faith, you are not likely to adopt their beliefs now. Those clichés could trigger a spiritual crisis. I was angry with God for quite some time. I felt like I was being punished, and I couldn't understand what I had done to deserve this tragedy. One of the worst clichés was "you're young. You can remarry," which was the farthest thing from my mind.

When I was still working, I would find things on my desk left by the board president…a card, a flower, an apple. I knew she cared but finding her gifts began to feel like thoughtful mouse droppings and that maybe she was avoiding me, which some friends did. One morning I found her sitting in my office. She said, "I hurt for you, but I hurt for myself also. If there is anything I can do for you, please tell me so I can do it, and we can both feel better." Nothing else needed to be said because she hugged me, and we cried together. I knew she was 'there' for me and not one of those folks who said, "Let me know if you need anything," as if I had the mental focus to think about what others could do for me. I did not care if the grass was mowed or if the house was cleaned.

Evenings and weekends were my worst times because those had been 'our' special time together. I walked and drove miles and miles, trying to grasp reality or perhaps run from it.

I worried about how we would survive economically and if I could raise my boys alone without their father. We squeezed by on our tight budget, but I wanted them to go to college, and I knew I could not afford to be a stay-at-home mom forever. I was obsessed with who I was and what I could do for the rest of my life.

Now that death had destroyed our family, I accepted that all people die. I didn't fear my death. At times I would have welcomed it. I feared the loss of my sons.

I had trouble being around certain people. I found that I resented women who complained about their husbands (while mine was deceased) or parents who mistreat their children...or just about any frivolous complaint that involved not being grateful for their lives. I found my circle of friends and even family getting smaller and smaller as I tried to come to grips with my life. The primary issue was finding people who didn't give me advice or think they had a right to tell me how to live my life. My circle of friends and family that were emotionally 'safe' to have around dwindled.

I came to view the emotional pain of my loss as a brick wall, and I tried to focus my emotional pain on one issue or brick at a time. The biggest rock on my wall consumed me. I dwelled on whether or not Joe suffered, how much he suffered, how intensely he suffered, how long he laid there by himself, and whether or not he was afraid to die. When I couldn't let these issues go, I visited the coroner, who explained Joe's injuries. Knowing he died instantly helped me to move that huge rock aside eventually. It didn't happen all at once, nor did I intentionally sit down and address the issue. My mind would just focus on it at various times. I realized later it was like visiting the big rock, with a rock hammer and a chisel and chipping small pieces away. Gradually the pain diminished, and I thought of his suffering less often. When I understood that his awareness of pain was only moments and he moved immediately into the light, I could accept the circumstances of his death.

I wondered if I would ever be happy again. My childhood was not particularly painful, but there was little time to play because I grew up in a large, hardworking, low-income family. Joe was fun-loving and full of life. He brought the happiest into my life. After his death, coping with daily life issues was exhausting for me. Just getting Billy off to school drained all my energy. Unlike before Joe's death, I took no interest in the house after his death. I seemed to cope best emotionally after I had been physically active. I had a half-acre lot at the new house, which I had fenced so the boys could play safely. Joe's dad wanted me to buy a riding lawn mower, but I refused his suggestion which was a big step for me. Normally I would do whatever Dad said because I didn't have the energy to argue. For example, when he said he didn't feel safe with the boys riding in my VW beetle with me, he ordered me a new Chevy station wagon. I picked out the color. I paid for it and sold the beetle to my best friend. But yard work was physical and something I enjoyed, so I bought a self-propelled lawn mower. I decided to plant a vegetable garden and had a farmer plow it with his tractor. Watching him bring the tractor into my yard was hard, but I did it. I also bought a small tiller at the local hardware store whose employee put the machine together. Something was wrong with it. It wouldn't dig. I loaned it to a friend who brought it back and said he couldn't use it. Years later, when I moved to Tennessee to get my doctorate, another friend borrowed it and brought it back with the same response. Together we looked at the manual that came with it, and even my friend Jack could not figure out what was wrong. I looked down at it and realized the tines were on backward. What a revelation! I had not solved the problem, but I had done something like that without Joe's help. He was the mechanical problem solver in the family. Gradually, I learned who I could rely on to help me problem solve, what I could do myself, and what we had to live without.

Writing in a journal, walking, driving, gardening, reading about grief, or talking to a safe person helped me survive. The realization that I needed to be the best parent I could be for the boys drove me to do things with them that many mothers would be afraid to do. I took them fishing and camping, and we really enjoyed those times. I was terrible at football. I always lobbed the ball and could never make it twirl. I also valued family involvement, so Joe's parents saw the boys often and took Billy on camping vacations or fishing with them. Uncle Lee took Billy fishing but said he couldn't manage Chris. My brother Charles and his wife Nancy spent special time with the boys through the years. I realized that I would die someday, and they were to be the boys' legal guardians. It was important that they develop a comfortable relationship with my brother and his wife. Years later, we would lose both Charles and Nancy at age 49 and one year apart.

Through my grief work, I clarified what was most important to me. I learned to savor my time with my children, family, and friends. What was most important to me was not what I owned, how much I earned, or how people in the community recognized me but the loving bonds I had formed with family and friends. I learned to say I love you at every opportunity.

I learned to be self-sufficient, to be a single parent, to problem solve alone, to cope with loneliness, and to do things I didn't think I could do. I focused on Joe's positive traits, but eventually, his stubborn streak had to be faced. Clearly, Joe's stubborn streak and resistance to mine and his father's suggestions was the cause of his death.

I did not think of myself in positive ways. Joe's reflection of his views of me were gone. I could not imagine being happy again. I studied affirmations. I put them in Billy's lunch box. I posted them on sticky notes around the house. I am loveable. I am capable. I am worthy. At first, the pain was so great that I could not see or accept those things. Gradually, my self-esteem and self-acceptance grew because he loved me.

As I was struggling to pull a new self-image of myself together, I had a call one night from a drunk man. He wanted to 'service' my sexual needs. I hung up. I became extremely anxious and more reluctant to go out for any reason. Somehow, I knew that man and wondered what on earth I had done that might have encouraged him to call. NOTHING! I eventually realized who he was, and he never looked me in the eyes again.

Joe was mechanically inclined, and I depended on him to take care of things. After his death, it seemed that all mechanical equipment died, beginning with Joe's van. I left it in the yard and did not drive it for months. When I did, the oil was thick because it had not been changed, and I blew the engine. Despite spending a lot of money on rebuilding it, oil leaks were a common problem. I finally sold it and gave an honest description of the problem. Household appliances died one after the other. When the washer wouldn't spin out the water, I called a friend to help me diagnose the problem. There was no such thing as 'YouTube' and the internet then. He explained that I needed to call a repairman and gave me the names of several, and encouraged me to wring out the clothes before the repairman arrived. I actually felt like I competently handled that problem with his input which I did not consider his advice. Advice is someone telling you what you 'should' or 'could' do. Even if they preface their advice with "If I were in your place, I would," it still is advice-giving. I learned to grow my own competencies for coping with life. I learned that people who do things for you without asking are caretakers (like Joe's well-meaning dad). He needed to feel better, and taking care of the boys and me was his way of coping with the loss of his son.

Life is sometimes filled with tacky, frustrating, frivolous details. Problems and other irritating tasks had a way of appearing when I felt least able to handle them. The first anniversary of Joe's death was totally unexpected to me. At the time, I did not understand that reliving the real nightmare weeks before the death was normal. When the death occurred, I was not numb. But during the first anniversary, my feelings were raw and intense. I thought I could not survive. I learned later that anniversaries for trauma deaths are intense for several years. It's a big rock in your mountain of pain.

When Joe died, I was faced with deciding 'who I was' and 'how I would get on with my life'. Certainly, I had enough people telling me that I needed to get on with my life. I could not grasp that each day was a new beginning. It was also the only day I had. The past was gone, and our future was unpredictable. Learning to live in the present, one day at a time, allowed me to experience my life more fully. It was hard to do, but I learned to focus on enjoying the present moment. Slowly I learned to breathe my way through my anxiety about the future.

During my grief work, I was not looking for opportunities for personal insight and growth because I was afraid to face myself. Eventually, I realized that nothing from the past was so terrible that I could not grow beyond it. Whatever issues surfaced as I conducted my life review, I learned to handle them, and as I did, my coping skills improved.

My friend Liz's sister came for a visit at Christmas the second year after Joe's death, and she stayed with us in Billy's room. She had been there several days and was about to leave when she decided to tell me about an experience she had. She was awakened by the bedroom being filled with bright light, and she saw Joe standing at the foot of the bed. She had never met him, but she realized that she knew who he was. He asked her if she knew him and if she was afraid. She realized she was not afraid. Then he told her he needed her to give me a message. He wanted me to have a good Christmas. I never questioned her story but wondered why he could not have come to me. Then I recognized that I would have been so traumatized by having to give him up again when I woke.

The New Year holiday was very difficult for several years. I felt like I had nothing to celebrate. I was filled with dread about living another painful year. I made no resolutions.

The third task of mourning is adjusting the roles, responsibilities, and tasks that have to be completed which had been fulfilled by the deceased. I learned how to take care of the car and who to ask for advice when something needed to be fixed. It was the personal things that Joe did with me and the boys that no one could fill. Uncle Lee took Billy fishing, and Billy's reaction was fishing wasn't fun without Daddy.

I began thinking about what kind of new career I needed as a single parent. Teaching would allow me to have summers free. My favorite college professor was a health educator, so I began looking into universities that offered that type of degree. My master's degree was in health education, so that seemed a logical decision. I felt that I had to take charge of my own life.

Chapter Three: Moving Forward With Life

I decided to continue my education, researched the best graduate school program, applied to the University of Tennessee in Knoxville, and was accepted. I announced my decision to Joe's Mon and Dad and promptly had a visit from Joe's brother Lee who told me that taking the kids away from his parents was selfish of me. I tried to explain that I needed a way to earn money, and his answer was you are doing okay. My response was yes, we are getting by, but what happens when the social security ends and the boys need to go to college? His response was you can get a job then. My thoughts were I would have been out of the workforce too long then, and what kind of job would I qualify for at that point? Mom and Dad never objected to my getting my doctorate.

I applied for a graduate teaching assistantship and was awarded it, so my tuition was waived. I applied for graduate student housing, and we were assigned an apartment. Our house in Berea was offered to Liz and Glenn, who agreed to take care of our dog Benji, so we packed what we needed and moved. Billy was enrolled in an elementary school, and I found a reliable babysitter for Chris. The biggest issue I had to face was my own insecurity. Was I smart enough? Could I manage parenting, housekeeping, cooking, a full-time load of classes, and teaching? My planning and organization skills were functioning again, and I learned to let less important things go. I passed the courses, surprisingly, class by class, with all As and one B. There were only 9 of us in the program, and I was the only single parent.

My dissertation research was on adjustment to bereavement. I found a local funeral home that helped me find widows to be in my study. Reading now was focused on research articles and not self-help, and it was amazing to me how much I learned. The first chapter of my dissertation introduced the need for my research. In our research class, our writing was critiqued by three classmates to whom we had to present and defend what we had written orally. One male student was particularly harsh in his written and verbal comments to my chapter. I was questioning my competency when the professor said, "Judy, why don't you write this chapter from your personal experience?"

The critical male student responded, "What do you mean?"

My answer was, "Wayne, I am a widow."

His face showed emotion, and he said, "I thought you were divorced." He tried to be nicer to me after that, but I knew he was not a safe person. So, what if I had been divorced? I was still a single parent trying to start a new career so I could provide for myself and my children.

The boys and I went back to Berea as often as we could, but my responsibilities made that infrequent. We talked to Mom and Dad regularly by phone. Dad got sick with a lung infection, and we rushed back home. A few days later, when we were back in Knoxville, we got the call that Papa Keith had died. Another loss, another thing on my full plate that needed my attention, and another loss for my sons who loved their Papa. I trudged onward, one class at a time.

I was in my second year of graduate school when I met Gary, a non-traditional student who took my first-aid class. He was good-looking and intelligent. I was a competent and committed teacher. In reading one of his required assignments, he included an off-the-wall commit about a snake bite to see if I actually read my student's assignments. My written comment was I hate snakes. We had a good laugh about that later. After the semester was over, he asked me out. I was quite surprised by his attention but felt ready to reinvest in living in that part of my life. He gave attention to the boys, and we had fun weekends together. His family lived across town, and since he worked and went to school, I assumed the infrequent contact was due to time constraints. I did not see the red flag. Christmas came during the last year of graduate school, and we were all invited to his mom's and dad's house. His sister and her kids were there. His mother bought small gifts for the grandchildren but not for my boys. It was awkward when gifts were opened, and my boys were left out. Gary was furious and confronted his mother. She complained that his father had not given her enough money to buy the boys gifts. Gary told her then she should not have invited us. His Dad left and went downstairs to his 'man cave'. I did not see the red flag. We did not visit them again. Gary was director of a halfway house for recovering alcoholics in Oak Ridge, Tennessee. He had served as a marine in Vietnam. His undergraduate degree in psychology was completed at the same time I finished my doctorate. He applied for certification from the State of Tennessee to be a drug and alcohol counselor in preparation for his move with us to a new location. He reported his own drinking habits honestly and was turned down for drug counseling certification by the state. Another red flag was missed because my knowledge of addiction was limited. I thought he would know with all his work experience when he was in trouble with alcohol.

My dissertation was complete, my coursework finished, and my oral defense was successful. I was Dr. Judy Keith. To me, it was an accomplishment that was meant to give us some security. All that was left for me was to find a job. I had two offers. One was from Austin Pea University in Tennessee, and the other was from the University of New Orleans. We chose New Orleans.

Chapter Four: Loss of a Marriage

The boys and I packed our clothes, the dog, birds, and fish, and looked a little like the Beverly Hillbillies in our station wagon. I rented a house in Slidell, Louisiana, and when we arrived, a woman came out to greet me, offer me ice tea, and welcome us to the neighborhood. She had an unusual accent, and I am sure she thought I did as well, so I asked her where she was from. Her answer was Algiers which I thought was a foreign country, not a community across the river! Getting accustomed to Louisiana's dialects, customs, food, and communities would be fun. Gary quit his job and came weeks later.

I started my job at the University of New Orleans and, overall, had a good work experience. There were some folks who liked to play their version of politics and abuse of power, but they did not prevent me from doing my job. I taught, advised students, published, worked on grants, and moved slowly up the pay scale. I co-authored a small college-level textbook on death and dying and also worked as a consultant on a large federal cardiovascular disease grant at Louisiana State University. We needed all the extra income I could make.

Gary was at a loss as to what he wanted to do with his own career, so after much discussion, we decided to open a craft store in the French Quarter. It seemed like a good decision as crafts had always been one of my interests, and he had lived in Knoxville during the World's fair there and saw the economic benefits. We used my money, of course, and he was to run the shop. We did not know that shortly after we opened the gallery, the streets and sidewalks in the French Quarter would be torn up and replaced. Many old and new businesses had to close during the reconstruction. Gary began isolating himself in his 'office' above the garage. I did not know what he was brooding about, but multiple beers were his daily beverage. One night I found him with a gun in his hand. He ordered me to leave. I took the boys and left but called his dad, thinking he might be able to talk him out of his plan to end his life. He did, but it was hours later before the boys, and I could come home. I never told them what he had threatened to do. One day he refused to go to work and said he wanted to go to graduate school instead. I lost a bundle of money but closed the shop and dispensed the remaining merchandise.

During the time the shop was open, Mama Keith and Gary's father, Howard, came to visit us during Mardi Gras. Howard exhibited no noticeable signs of alcoholism at that time, of my limited knowledge. After all, he and Gary only drank beer. Gary's mother and father had divorced, and his mother remained in the house while Howard lived in a trailer. Gary was halfway through his masters in arts at Louisiana State University, while I supported him when Howard strangled to death on a binge drunk. When we visited his trailer, beer and ketchup were the only things we found in his refrigerator. The families' interactions during the funeral gave me stark insights into their dysfunction. His sister lamented about what Howard had done to her, one brother, who was well on his way to addiction, came drunk, and the third one, who was homeless, did not come to the funeral. I learned that as a teenager, the homeless brother chose to live in the barn instead of the house with his family. Gary seemed okay during the funeral but showed little emotion. I assumed that was because he was the eldest child. As months passed and the feud over his father's limited estate erupted, he became sullen and more withdrawn. He began to draw dark and scary pictures as an outlet for his pain. He was angry all the time. A friend who visited us who had a mental health background examined his drawings and advised me not to do anything to upset him. His drinking increased, and he was usually already drunk by the time he returned home from school.

One day Billy and Chris had been playing one of his old records without his permission. He lost it with them. Billy went to his room, and Gary followed him. I assumed he intended to lecture him until I heard his belt hit Billy, who let out a yelp. I froze and did not understand why. The following year, I recovered memory of my dad using a belt on my brother Charles when we were young and recognized the experience as my original trauma. I suddenly returned to the present and raced up the stairs, only after Billy had been given several harsh blows. I grabbed Billy and told Gary if he ever touched him again, I would kill him. Chris told me years later that when the old dishwasher did not clean the dishes, he whipped both of them and made them wash the dishes by hand.

We discussed going to therapy, and after only one appointment, Gary said he was smarter than the therapist. I gave him another chance to find a therapist he could accept. I also gave him an ultimatum. Either stay in therapy or get out of our lives.

The boys were allowed to go visit their Mama Keith, who was a treat for them and a relief for me. While with her, Billy talked to his grandmother about Gary. Joe's oldest brother, Eugene, called to tell me I was not a good mother. I didn't need his advice or interference. I knew we were in a perilous place and was doing my best to get us out of it.

Our therapist was a female with a masters in social work. Billy had his own male therapist. I liked them both. When Gary failed to keep his appointment with the therapist, the boys and I continued ours. I asked Gary to leave the house. He took some clothes and my car and left. He took my car because the payment came out of my paycheck automatically. His van had to be paid directly by check. To protect my credit rating, I continued paying the van payment. We had very little contact with him. He claimed he was living in the Toyota Tercel, which I knew for a man his size to be impossible. I later learned he was living with his next 'sugar mama'. I found a lawyer who wrote him a letter ordering him to return my car and take the van. He did so while I was at the University. However, I still had to pay for the van to protect my credit rating. I filed for divorce. One night while I was teaching a class, he kicked in the back door and threatened the boys who locked themselves in Billy's upstairs bedroom and climbed down their fire escape ladder. They hid in the woods until he left. He broke into the hall closet where I had locked his guns for safety and took those and the remainder of his personal things.

From that point forward, I came home to get my sons and took them back with me to teach my night class. They used the time to do their school work and play games with each other. I could focus on what I had to do because I knew they were safe. Billy was seventeen and a half and trustworthy with Chris. To ease the time pressure of driving back and forth from New Orleans to Pearl River, which was 35 miles away, I gave Billy a Toyota pickup. He had a part-time job at McDonald's, was in the high school band, and had a girlfriend. It seemed like the practical thing to do. He loved that little navy-blue truck that he had been driving for six weeks.

Chapter Five: Loss of a Child

It was Sunday, September 28, 1987. The boys and friends played football in the sideyard. I made a pot of chili for the kids to eat after playing. Billy had to take his girlfriend, Cecilia, home, so he asked me not to let Chris go with him because he had something he needed to talk to her about. A short time later, I got a call from someone who said Billy was in an accident and I needed to come quickly. Chris and I drove down Military Road, where the accident occurred. His truck was sitting beside the road, and the ambulance had already taken him to Slidell Hospital. We drove as fast as we could to the hospital. When I got to the emergency room registration area to identify myself as his mother, I could see him on a bed through the open door, and he was having a seizure. I passed out.

I kept going to the desk asking for information and got nothing. After what seemed like hours, the emergency room doctor came out and took me into a small room where he told me Billy's injuries were really serious and he did not think he would make it. I was allowed to see him. He was unconscious. Then a neurosurgeon was brought in to do surgery to elevate the fracture in his skull. After the surgery, he told us to go home and get some rest. I hated to leave

Billy, but we did as we were told. Friends Janice and Gerry Bodet were at our house. They took care of Chris and answered the phone throughout the hospital stay. The call came from the hospital thirty minutes later, asking us to come back to the hospital. We did. The neurosurgeon wanted permission to remove blood clots from his brain. After that surgery, I never left the hospital.

Billy's friends came, but only one parent came, and she talked inappropriately in front of the kids about Billy's possible handicaps if he even lived. Cecilia, his girlfriend, was beside herself, often running from the waiting room to hide from the hospital social worker who came to talk to the teenagers. Cecilia told me if that clammy-handed social worker tried to talk to her again, she was going to stuff tissue down her mouth. No one came from either of my sons' schools. I kept Billy's friends informed of what little information was given to me. Mama Keith, Uncle Lee, my brother Charles and his wife Nancy were on their way from Kentucky and Virginia to Louisiana. Two days later, the neurosurgeon asked for permission to remove part of the frontal lobe of Billy's brain to give him room to swell.

The consequence, if he lived, would be that we would have to teach him how to talk, walk, and use the bathroom again. Chris and I discussed it and agreed that we wanted him to live, and teaching him those things would be fine with us. That evening Janice and Gerry came to the hospital to visit. Gerry told me that he had a 'communication' from their daughter Jeanne who assured him Billy would be okay. Jeanne had died two years before in a car accident right after her wedding. We had never met her. I sat in the waiting room with my friend Melanie, praying, meditating, and trying to send Billy my life energy. Chris was asleep on the floor with a neighbor we called Big Eddy. After two and a half days of no sleep, I fell asleep sitting in the chair. Fifteen minutes later, I woke with the most profound peace filling my body, and I knew that Billy was gone. Then panic set in again, and I began praying. Melanie and Eddy came silently into the room. It was 3 am. The next morning around 8 am, I received a call from my friend Joe. The doctor came in to speak to me, and I just knew he was dead. I screamed and begged to have him back alive. After I calmed down, I was allowed to go into his room to see him. He looked peaceful, as if he was asleep. I touched his arm, and it was warm. I looked at his chest, which was rising and falling as if he were breathing, and I thought, "They have made a mistake. He is not dead." Then I looked at all the machines that kept his organs alive and realized he was gone. I went back out to the waiting room to talk to Chris, who was twelve years old at the time.

I explained the machines and the false idea that he was still alive. I took him back to see his brother, and he asked for some private time. Before Billy died, I took each of his friends back to see him. One by one, they, too, asked for private time to say goodbye. The doctor came in and asked about organ donation. Chris and I discussed it and agreed that would be Billy's wish. Mama Keith and Uncle Lee arrived, and soon after, my brother Charles and his wife, Nancy. Mama wanted to see Billy, as did Charles and Nancy. Gerry and Janice Bodet came, and Gerry was furious when he heard the news that Billy was dead. Two doctor friends came to the hospital, one an internationally known cardiologist. I asked these doctors when they thought the soul left the body and was told that Billy, as we knew and loved him, was gone. Melanie later told me that after I fell asleep in the chair, she felt a powerful urge to go into Billy's room. She said they knew he was leaving his body the minute they entered the room. The readings on his instruments changed, and the nurses came in to adjust them.

Since we had donated organs, they were not harvested until the morning after he died, which was my mother's birthday. She was heartbroken, as all of my and Joe's family were. Billy's friends were told to go home when we did but one friend, Colin, stayed until the organs were harvested and the machines disconnected. I did not know this until much later.

We were advised to go home to make funeral arrangements. I wrote a bereavement newsletter for a funeral home group that went to a huge mailing list in the New Orleans area. I called the owner of the funeral corporation to make arrangements. I wanted to use a church close enough to the schools so my sons' friends could walk to the service. Janice Bodet asked if she could lead the service, and even though she worked for the biggest competitor to the funeral home that was serving us, she was allowed to do so. Chris and I picked clothes for Billy to wear. Chris wanted him to look natural, not stuffy, so we picked khaki slacks and a summer shirt that Mama Keith had given him that said 'Bad Boys Surf Club' on the back. Chris wore his matching shirt and khaki slacks. I invited Billy's friends to come over and let them spend some time in his room. They discussed what they should wear as honorary pallbearers. I told them that whatever they wore was fine with me. They chose to go to the mall to buy black slacks, shirts, and skirts. I gave them permission to pick some of Billy's personal things to keep as a linking object. They were thoughtful in their choices. Cecilia wanted his glasses and blue jean jacket, and the boys picked fishing and hunting magazines. Edward came to me to ask if Billy would have any hair, and I told him it had been shaved and would be put in the casket at his feet in a plastic bag. He asked me if Billy could wear the Crescent City Classic painter's cap he had won when he finished the 6.2-mile race. It was put on his head. The friends were told to put the word out that they would be allowed to place personal items in the casket with Billy as a way of saying goodbye. Chris stuffed Billy's old ragged Peter Rabbit toy he'd had since he was an infant into the head of his own favorite stuffed Ronald McDonald toy. He also placed his football into the casket that Billy had gotten one of his high school friends to sign, who later played for the Detroit Lions. The band members, football players, and others put pictures of themselves in the casket with messages on the back. One friend gave me a letter she had written to Billy and put a copy in the casket for Billy. I respected Billy's classmate's privacy and read nothing that was not given to me too. The church was standing room only with others outside in the churchyard. Billy's high school principal spoke, and it was obvious he knew nothing about my son. His and Chris's junior high principal spoke next, and his comments were right on and thoughtful.

Mine and Chris' therapist sat in the pew right behind us at the funeral. Chris' best friend sat beside him. My divorce attorney called before the funeral to tell me that Gary wanted to attend. Since he had adopted the boys shortly after we married, he had a legal right. The attorney also said if I did not want him to come, he would fight like hell to keep him away. He was not present. Gary did write me a letter which was more an explanation of his actions than an apology. I burned it.

The music I wanted to be played for the benefit of the kids was *Lean on Me* by Bill Withers, but the minister objected. I offered him a more modern rock version, and again he objected. Finally, one of my university students who practiced flute with Billy found a version sung by Johnnie Mathis, and the minister finally accepted it. My intention was for the song to be a supportive message for the kids, but their reaction to it was that it described Billy. My university student played Billy's flute at his funeral. The students appreciated the music.

As families who live far away always do, ours left after Billy was declared brain dead. The remains were transported to Kentucky by plane after the Louisiana funeral. Melanie had to fly up and did not know Billy was on the plane too. As she descended the airplane's steps, she saw a shooting star, and as her eyes followed it down toward the grounds, she saw them bringing Billy's coffin out of the hold. She said she felt like she was bringing him home. A shooting star is symbolic of a released soul.

The second funeral in Berea was for family and friends. I remember little of it except that my friend Joe practically held me up as I greeted the line of people who came. He kept putting cards I was given in his coat pocket. When it was over, the funeral home gave me a bill for services which also went into his pocket. I realized that the Louisiana funeral home had not given me a bill. Colleagues from the University had donated money, and I was later told that the funeral home donated the rest. The day after his funeral in Kentucky, I searched through the cards but could not find the bill. I called Joe. He said, "let me check my jacket, and I'll get back to you." Sometime later, he called to tell me he did not want me to be upset, but he and a couple of my friends paid the bill. I was to speak no more about it.

I shared this information with Mama Keith, whose response was, "He really is your friend, isn't he."

A colleague from the University had driven us to Berea. Several of Billy's friends came with us to the second funeral. I do not remember where the young people and my colleague stayed. Nor do I remember driving home.

My sister, Nina, who had stayed with us when Billy was born, stayed with us for a week after Billy's funeral. I have no memory of how she got to Louisiana. She cooked, washed clothes, and cleaned and cleaned, which was her way of coping. One day as she was heading up the stairs with clean linen, I said, "Sis, I feel like a lousy housekeeper because all you have done since you've been here is clean." She gave me one of 'those' looks and proceeded up the stairs.

When she came downstairs, she said, "I don't know how you are dealing with this because it is killing me. Leave me alone because I can clean." The neighbors asked if she was available to help them.

I had to return to work. My department chair thoughtfully brought Janice Bodet to teach the rest of the semester of the death and dying class. Toward the end of the semester, Janice asked me to come to speak to the students. I talked with them about Billy's death, and they gave me a large bouquet of flowers. I do not remember teaching any of my classes that semester, but years later, I had a former student in a workshop who said I was the best teacher she had at UNO. She was in one of my classes the semester Billy died.

My focus was on grieving and taking care of Chris, who was suicidal. We both stayed in therapy, and he had an anti-suicidal contract with the therapist. He came home from school one day to tell me he was proud of himself, which was an unusual comment. I asked him what had happened at school, and he said, "I didn't hit Ms. Sims!" I asked him what Ms. Sims had done that made him want to hit her. She had given him classwork to do, which he had started working on, but then his thoughts triggered to the decision we had made to remove part of his brother's brain. She noticed him not working, came up behind him, slapped him on the back, and told him loudly to get back to work. I called his principal, described the event, and told him I needed an appointment to talk with her. He asked me to speak to all of Chris' teachers. I saved my talk with her for last. None of his teachers knew how to relate to Chris' pain or how to help him. When I introduced myself to Ms. Sims, I was simply Judy, Chris' mom, not the university professor with a doctorate who had co-authored a college-level death and dying textbook, taught a death and dying class or did research on bereavement.

I said, "Ms. Sims, I need you to call me when Chris is having a bad day."

In an annoyed voice, she said, "I don't have time to call parents."

I said, "Ms. Sims, I assume you know that Chris recently lost his brother. He also lost his dad when he was two and a half and his grandfather after his father's death. His dog was also killed. He is in therapy two times a week and is suicidal. I need you to call me when he has had a difficult day so the therapist and I can support him."

She said, "Well, you seem to be doing alright. When is he going to be okay?" I was proud of myself also because I really wanted to hit the bitch!

Instead, I paused. Finally, I looked her in the eyes and asked, "Ms. Sims, have you ever lost anyone close to you?"

She said, "Yes," and I saw the pain in her eyes.

I asked, "How long did it take you to be okay?"

She said, "About a year and a half," which told me one of two things. Either she had not been very close to the person who died, or more likely, she had been very close and did not have supportive people who allowed her to grieve. Since she was so uncomfortable with Chris, I assumed the latter was true.

It was only October, and the remainder of the year did not improve for Chris. None of the teachers called me, but Chris talked to me and his therapist. I told him not to worry about grades because he could repeat the year at another school. He was doing more important grief work.

Chris developed enlarged lymph nodes throughout his body. The pediatrician referred him to an oncologist for further evaluation. I could not breathe; my fear was so intense. We were given an early appointment, and when we arrived, the receptionist said the doctor would be right with us. She called me by my doctor title. I sat down thinking I did not normally use my title, but perhaps I had when I made the appointment. We were immediately taken back to the doctor's personal office, not an exam room. The doctor greeted us warmly and shook Chris' hand. He introduced his nurse and asked Chris, 'man-to-man', if he could go with the nurse to have some blood drawn without his mom. They left the room. Then the young doctor turned a picture around on his desk of a teenage boy. He said, "I want to thank you for the newsletter you wrote about Billy's death and funeral. It helped my family when my brother was killed in a car accident two weeks after Billy." We both shed a few tears, and then it was back to seeing what Chris needed done. He told me that it was not likely that he had anything seriously wrong because he was under so much stress. Most likely, his immune system was under attack, and the enlarged nodes were his body's defense. He expedited the blood work results and called me himself to give me the good news. Again, he said, "Thank you for helping others."

Billy's friends were still hurting. Cecilia spent many nights with us, sleeping in his room and writing poetry on his computer. She struggled with guilt because she had given him alcohol, and the last words he said to her were, "I love you."

The last thing she said to him was, "I'm not sure I know what love is, but I know you're my best friend." He got in his truck and did not fasten his seat belt. He went to a store one mile away to get her a coke and cigarettes. He was not speeding when he hit trash in the roadway. Someone had weed eaten the ditch line and thrown the trash on the road. The lady in the car behind him said he hit the trash and tried to pull onto the shoulder when his truck flipped, and he was thrown out of it. According to witnesses, he was asking for help before he began having seizures. For me, that he suffered, without me there, was a rock as big as a mountain.

Chris was upset because the accident was caused by trash on the road, so I suggested we could pick up roadside trash. His friends continued to stay in touch, so I organized a trash cleanup campaign. Every weekend, the kids and I picked up trash, and the mayor of Pearl River had it hauled away on Monday. Then they wanted to plant a garden in his memory. The mayor provided the railroad ties, soil, and plants, and the teenagers worked at the town's entrance. Then we planned a 'Festival of Lights' at Christmas. The schools were asked to have students make ornaments. The mayor got the biggest tree she could find and erected it in front of city hall. No one but her knew that I worked to honor my son.

Christmas for Chris and me was to start at our home, and then we would travel to see family. As we decorated the tree, Chris asked me what we would do with Billy's stocking. I had learned to ask him what he needed to do. He hung both their stockings on either end of the mantle. Then he asked what we were going to do with Billy's ornaments. Again, I asked him what he wanted to do. He methodically hung one of his and then one of Billy's on the tree. Christmas Eve came, and he said, "Mommy, I don't know if I can make it through the night by myself."

I said, "You won't be alone. I'm here."

He said, "Mommy did you really not know?"

I responded, "Not know what?"

He said, "Billy and I used to stay up all night. We would sneak downstairs, and he would take a package into the closet, open it to see what it was, and then rewrap it." In the past, my breakfast was always ready at the crack of dawn every Christmas morning because our rule was we had to eat before opening presents. Billy would cook the eggs and make coffee. Chris made toast and set the table. So, I told him I would be there for him if he needed me. I went to bed reluctantly, leaving my door open. I did not sleep through the night and often heard him up. He never came to my room. Once I heard him crying and got up to go to him, but then I realized that if I did that, my actions would convey to him that he needed me to make it. I sat down on the stairs, cried, and went back to bed. The next morning when he came to get me, breakfast was ready. He had never made scrambled eggs before, and they were rubbery. The coffee was really strong. The toast was hard as a rock, but I ate everything with gratitude. We opened our presents, but there was no celebration or joy. We carried his gifts upstairs to his room. In the walk-in closet floor, he had spread a baby blanket made by Grandma Bryant when Billy was born. Our family picture album was open in front of a framed picture of Billy, which was sitting on his dad's Bible. He had reviewed his life with Billy, but more importantly, he had proven to himself that he could survive the night alone.

Mardi Gras was coming up, and like every little town around New Orleans, our town of Pearl River had a small parade. The chief of police loaned me his personal truck so that Billy and Chris' teenage friends could have a float in the parade. I obtained donated trash bags and literature on recycling and purchased daffodil bulbs. It was very cold for February. The kids kept taking turns sitting in the idling truck to get warm. Chris decided to play a game with Cecilia and kept locking the doors. He accidentally knocked the truck out of gear, and it rolled into a station wagon. Every cop in town was there within minutes. Repairs (which were probably not even made) on the old station wagon cost me a thousand bucks.

My divorce from Gary was final six weeks after Billy died. Chris wanted to go to court and tell the judge how he treated us. His counselor said to let him go. She knew he would not be allowed to speak. Gary came and with him was his latest conquest. He had been staying with her since leaving our house. Chris wanted to talk to her to warn her about what he was like. I assured him that she would not believe a word we said. She would eventually get mistreated by him too. The divorce was granted, and Gary was not allowed to see Chris until he returned to therapy and was approved for visitation. He never did. I was left with all the bills because Gary claimed he had no income. His inheritance from his dad's estate did not come to light until the IRS contacted me a year later.

Until Billy's death, I lived with the false belief that because I had lost Joe, I had some kind of insurance policy that would protect me from other losses. How naive of me. All people die, and I was determined I was not going to lose my other child.

My biggest rocks in Billy's grief wall were that he suffered, and I was not there to help him. The pain was so unbearable, and despite the issue coming up frequently, it was excruciating.

Eight years later, just before Easter, I was sitting in church listening to the sermon. The minister talked about Christ's suffering and his mother, Mary, having to watch him suffer and be unable to stop the pain or prevent him from dying. Suddenly I felt a presence, and the most profound peace filled my body. Yes, my son had suffered, but I accepted that he was at peace and experiencing unconditional love. Sometime later, during a workshop, I shared that story, and a Catholic priest asked me who I thought that presence was. Without hesitation, I said, "Mother Mary." When I think about the issue of Billy's suffering now, it is still painful, but rather than overwhelming, it is more like a dull ache.

My second biggest rock was that Gary had hit my children. I thought about finding him and killing him. I thought about how I would do it. Chris had the same issue. I had apologized to Billy before his death and to Chris numerous times since. Billy told me he forgave me, but somehow that was not enough to ease my pain. I made an appointment with Billy's counselor to discuss the issue with him. He assured me that Billy had forgiven me. To this day, that issue still bothers me. While I no longer want to kill Gary, I also believe that he has done no recovery work.

Chapter Six: Protecting Chris

I decided to move Chris closer to family and began searching for a job close to Southwest Virginia or Kentucky. There was a position at East Tennessee State University in Johnson City, TN, about two hours from my family in Virginia. Despite being warned by some of my colleagues that there were internal problems there, I ignored the red flags and took the job. The warnings were well deserved. The staff was furious because the existing chair had been removed, and his pick for the position had been overlooked to hire me instead. There were conflicts between two departments, and the wife of the chair of the other department was a faculty member in my department.

Furthermore, the new dean was a black woman who everyone resented. In addition, the newly hired graduate school director was a womanizer who had been fired from his previous position for financial malfeasances with grant funds. He was also having an affair with a graduate student and laughingly told me her husband burned his house just before he left town to take the Tennessee job. I had contacted his colleague from my graduate program at the previous university where he worked and was told to be on guard. The faculty was not a supportive group of people. Only one older man was pleasant to me, always stopping by my office to say good morning. The former chair invited me to lunch which I tried to view as positive, but we ate lunch at Taco Bell because he had some free coupons. One day when a female faculty member came into my office to speak to me, she realized I was crying and later brought me a piece of homemade pie for lunch.

After moving into the townhouse we rented, I registered Chris at the junior high to repeat seventh grade. I asked for an appointment with the principal, counselor, and all his teachers. They were all women. When we met, they were seated at a round table which gave me a little hope that things would be different for Chris. I introduced myself as Chris' mom, gave his background, told them he was repeating the grade and asked them to devise a plan for how they would support him. They agreed that he would be given a hall pass to see the counselor anytime he got upset. If she were busy, the principal would see him until the counselor was free. All the teachers agreed to call me if he had a difficult day. My next move was to find us counselors. He and I had an understanding that if he did not like the counselor, we would continue looking. He was uncomfortable with the first counselor, so I found Harry for him. Chris thought Harry was awesome. I found myself a counselor who specialized in codependency. Before leaving Louisiana, my counselor asked me why I picked Gary and who was his role model from my childhood. I did not pick Gary. He picked me. I did not understand why I accepted him. I began reading everything I could get my hands on regarding adult children of alcoholics (which Gary was), and my dad was as well. My father's father was a veteran of WW II and had been a binge drinker.

The real estate company I contracted with rented our house in Louisiana, so the mortgage was covered, and Chris was not happy in the townhouse we rented in Johnson City. We found a little cabin in the country that he fell in love with, so I bought it despite a tight budget. My focus was on him, and the job had my attention only when I was at work. After he went to sleep, I grieved, read, and journaled. I wasn't sleeping much, and my size three clothes hung on me. Finally, I made an appointment with an internist. I was diagnosed with PTSD and given an anti-depressant. It worked, and I began sleeping better immediately.

The so-called professionals at work continued with their back-biting conflict. I did my best not to engage in any of it. Interestingly enough, the womanizer was the only person at work who reached out to Chris and me in a supportive way. He invited Chris to spend the day on his farm deer hunting.

Bruce and I did not socialize at work or out of work. One day we met the chair of the dental department, Dr. Brooks, for lunch at a restaurant in the Holiday Inn. Afterward, we raced back for our meeting with the dean. Later that afternoon, I received a call from her secretary telling me the dean wanted to see me. She screamed at me about a possible sexual harassment charge because the director of the graduate program worked under me! She listened to nothing I said. I was fired from my position as chair of the department. The former chair was put back in charge, and I was assigned to a different office. I taught my classes and went home to my son, choosing not to interact with anyone. It was apparent that someone had seen us coming out of the Holiday Inn and jumped to conclusions. I really did not care what people thought because I knew the truth. The dean of the medical school called me to his office because our department was under his control. He wanted to assure me that I would have a teaching job for the following year. I had not even thought of that but told him I would not be staying. He asked me if I had another position, and I told him no. He asked me why I wouldn't consider staying as a faculty member. My answer was that I could not survive in a rattlesnake pit with two-headed snakes. He offered to give me a reference. I never used it. Instead, I opened an office and began marketing adult life-skills development classes. Before I could leave the university, someone invaded my office and tried to download a grant I had written. Since the grant was written for schools in Tennessee, I gave it to a colleague at the University of Tennessee in Chattanooga. It was funded by him and did not benefit the thief who attempted to steal it. What was more devastating was that that same thief stole the personal journal I used to grieve my son, my marriage, and my childhood.

Chris had made a new friend and was doing well in school. He needed a math tutor but soon caught up with his classmates. He looked forward to seeing his counselor, so things were beginning to calm down in our lives.

After a few months, my counselor admitted to me that she thought I was further along in my recovery work than she was, so she invited me to join a group she participated in composed entirely of therapists. That group was really helpful to me. I finally discovered that my role model for Joe was my favorite Uncle Wayne, and my dad, in his early years, was the role model for Gary.

I met the only friend I made while in Johnson City at an Adult Child of Alcoholics support group. Mary Ann decided she wanted to give me a gift for my birthday. She had a friend who did 'readings'. I was not only skeptical but also a little anxious about the idea. She said he was really good, and I agreed to see him as I did not want to offend her. Wes was a gentleman. We sat on his porch, and he handed me a deck of cards to shuffle. He said shuffling the cards allowed him to read my 'energy'. Then he began talking about Gary, whom I had described in a limited way to Mary Ann, so I assumed she had talked with him. Then he began telling me things that I had never discussed with anyone. Whoa! Then he said, "You've lost a son."

I said, "Yes."

He said, "I want you to know that he is okay, and he had a very good soul as his guide during his passage. Do you know who that was?"

I said, "His dad."

He said, "No, it was a female." One of my former students had died while we lived in Louisiana, and she spent a lot of time with us during her illness, so I said her name.

He said, "No." Then I remembered Gerry Bodet's conversation about Jeanne, and I said her name. Wes shivered, and goose bumps came up on his arms.

He said, "Yes, that is who it was."

When I called Gerry Bodet that evening, he cried and said, "Yes that is what Jeanne meant. I thought she meant he would live, but she told me she would take care of him."

A colleague from Kentucky contacted me about a teaching job at Morehead State University. Since I needed a steadier income than my classes generated, I applied and was hired. I had to sell the cabin in TN and find a place to live in Berea, where Mama Keith lived. Berea was 90 miles from Morehead. A neighbor bought the cabin, and I found a small house a few blocks from Mama Keith to rent. I commuted Chris back to Johnson City for his sessions with Harry, his counselor, until I found another one for him in Lexington who did cognitive-emotive therapy with him. Mama Keith's next-door neighbor had to go into a nursing home, and she asked me to rent her house so we could be closer to Mama. I jumped at the chance because I knew Chris would be safe until I got home from work. I gave him a golden retriever puppy for Christmas. He named him Arnold after the bodybuilder. He was also given a workshop at a body-building camp with Arnold himself, where he took a picture with him and met Lou Ferrigno and other bodybuilders. He was beginning to act like a normal teenager.

A friend of Chris' from childhood, whose mother and father had been my friends, insisted their son invite Chris to a campout he was having in the woods behind their house. The boy's grandmother was in charge during the day while the parents worked. Chris had been friends with this boy since early childhood, so he went but called me shortly afterward to come and get him. His 'friend' had taken alcohol from his dad's liquor cabinet, and the boys, minus Chris, were all drunk. The boys had shot bb and pellet guns at Chris.

After he turned sixteen, I gave him a red pickup with an extended cab. He had a paper route which gave him responsibility but little financial reward. His best friends at school became two boys who understood grief. One's dad had died of a heart attack, and the other's mom was dying of cancer. Eric, whose mother had cancer, spent many nights on my sofa because he struggled with his mom's impending death. After she died, he continued sleeping on my couch.

I was driving 180 miles each day to and from work, trying to be present for Chris when I got home, keeping the house clean and the yard mowed as best I could. I learned a lot from my children over the years about their needs. Chris taught me when he needed to talk. He would come home from school and say, "Mom, don't peel potatoes (or fold laundry or whatever). I need you to listen to me." He was my most important priority. He had a girlfriend whom he really liked. However, his so-called childhood friend spread gossip about them at school, and she broke up with him. It was a double whammy because he finally realized the boy really was not his friend. I came home one day to find him with his daddy's pistol, which I thought was hidden. I returned to panic mode, gave the pistol and the shotgun to friends to keep, and he spent more time with his counselor.

His second girlfriend in Berea lived across the street from us. She drove a sports car, and he wanted one too. He found a used 300ZX, and we traded his new truck for it. The car was fun to drive for a while. When his girlfriend broke up with him, he decided he wanted to live in our house in Louisiana and go to the University of New Orleans. His best friend in Louisiana would live with him and help pay expenses. I was leery about letting him go, but his counselor thought he had some things he needed to process by living there. I agreed and made it happen. He enrolled at UNO, and Randy moved in. However, Randy was a messy kid and not responsible about his share of the expenses. Chris got a job at a pizza place but did poorly in school. He met a girl there and decided he wanted to marry Teri. They came to Kentucky, had a wedding, found an apartment, and got jobs. However, Teri's two-year-old son from a previous relationship had nowhere to sit in the sports car, so I gave him my car and drove his. I was accused of overindulging him, and maybe I was guilty. The marriage did not last long, and Teri left him to go back to Louisiana. Like his mom before him, he was left to pay the bills they had accumulated.

Chris decided he wanted to return to college, enrolled at Eastern Kentucky University, and majored in computer science. He had a job at a pizza place. One of his best friends worked there and had a sister, and told Chris he needed to ask her out. Chris jokingly told him that he was not interested if she was as ugly as he was. When he finally did ask Lynette out, I think it was love at first sight. He came home walking on air and told me how beautiful she was. They did not marry until his degree was finished, and he quickly found a job. He was finally on the right track with his life. When Billy died, one of the commitments I made, in addition to putting Chris' needs first, was that I would someday end my career teaching school staff how to support children who experienced trauma and loss.

I was still teaching my classes at Morehead, had made some new friends in the community through hospice, and together we offered a grief workshop for school counselors. I also rewrote the grant I had given away, and four Kentucky school districts funded it. I hired a colleague from the University of Tennessee in Chattanooga to whom I had given a copy of the grant to be the evaluator for my grant because he was experienced with what we planned to accomplish. The chair of my department began refusing to sign off on requisitions for teaching materials and payments to the evaluator and left the unsigned requisitions on his desks for weeks. Only when we were behind schedule did I realize what he was doing. I often found things on my desk moved and began to suspect someone with a master key was riffling through my files. This behavior represented another boundary invasion that triggered me. My student secretary was a feisty young lady who suggested I sprinkle baking soda on the floor behind my desk to see if we could, in fact, prove I was not paranoid. The department chair left his footprints without even realizing what he had done. From that time forward, the student assistant walked my purchase requisitions through for signature, once even going to his class and boldly knocking on his door. I decided I would not work again with those kinds of dysfunctional behaviors so I contacted the US Department of Education and asked that the grant administration be transferred to one of the experimental schools. Although highly unusual, my request was granted. After the transfer was complete, I quit teaching at the end of the semester at Morehead State University. The hospice workshop I had assisted my friend in conducting led me to an opportunity to present a workshop to school staff in Ohio, so I began my consulting career in earnest. This simple beginning led me to assist school districts in writing and funding more than 100 federal grants and developing training materials for teaching school counselors, social workers, psychologists, administrators, nurses, teachers, and others about children experiencing grief and trauma. My workshops were presented to school districts in 42 states over a period of 32 years. The districts I trained in had experienced school shootings, 9/11, hurricanes Katrina and Rita, tornadoes and bus accidents where students were killed, and suicides by students and staff. In addition to being a mom, I think this work was my life purpose.

I could do this very difficult work because I had done my grief and trauma recovery work. When I had workshops in different states, back-to-back, with only one day to travel in between workshops, I would get forgetful. In fact, I forgot two workshops, and they had to be rescheduled. Because I sometimes teared up during the training, participants would ask if it helped me with my grief to do this kind of training. No, I could not have done the work if I had not spent years working through my own losses. However, the concept of closure, as if there is an end to grief work, is widely held and worth repeating here. I am always sad on the anniversary of

Billy's death, but I can also celebrate his life with his brother and me.

Because I had a strong professional reputation, I was also hired by a private foundation to teach a drug prevention curriculum, so financially, I was safe.

Chapter Seven: Grieving my Childhood

When I realized that Gary had picked me, that he was so unhealthy, but I could not see the red flags, I decided to grieve any issues from my childhood. I embarked on a portion of my journey that was painful, insightful, and helped me grow significantly. I started by reading books on co-dependency, attending Adult Children of Alcoholic conferences, listening to tapes purchased at those conferences, attending an ACOA group, counseling, participating in the therapist group, and writing in my journal. A list of some of the books I read, highlighted, wrote in the margins and journaled my way through are listed in the Appendix.

I described that portion of my recovery process in a workshop I presented at the International Death Conference in Canada in 1992. The workshop was titled

Growing Beyond Survival: Grief Experiences of Children from Dysfunctional Families. The gist of the workshop is presented here from my personal and educator's perspective.

I grew up in a large family of eight children. My mother also birthed a stillborn and miscarried once. I would describe my mother as struggling with depression for much of her life. My father was a coal miner for thirty-five years. He was the hero child of an alcoholic father. Both parents were children of poverty. My entire family worked very hard to survive. Each child was expected to contribute to child care, household chores, care of farm animals, and gardening. We raised and preserved the majority of our food supply. Because of the large family, the limited resources, and the necessity of work, emotional nurturing and many developmental needs and tasks were inadequately met. Since both of my parents were reared in similar circumstances, their parenting skills were also limited. Mom carried out discipline with a switch you had to cut yourself, and by Dad with a belt. Mom frequently threatened us with the "Wait till your dad gets home" message. As far as I can remember, Dad only whipped my brother Bob and my brother Charles once with a belt.

While reading about dysfunctional families, I understood that a dysfunctional family involves multi-generational issues, including those who wounded and nurtured us. Uncle Wayne was the only male in my life who loved us unconditionally. He was my role model for Joe. After Joe's death and five years later, I married a man like my father again. Gary was the hero child of an alcoholic whose degree in psychology was an effort to help himself. My father, like

Gary, was the hero in his dysfunctional family. When his sister's husband drank too much, Mom and Dad and his father, Pa George, would take food, clothes, and coal to her family to get them through the winter. My dad only missed a day of work when he was injured in the coal mine and always took any overtime that was available. He was a good provider but lacked emotional and nurturing skills. Mom was nurturing but overwhelmed with too many children and tasks, including growing and preserving as many vegetables as we could. The children all learned to be responsible by helping her.

It was my own co-dependent trying to "fix" Gary which led me to understand that my choice in the second husband was to fulfill a "hunger attachment" created by my emotionally unavailable father. The "observer's" position I held in analyzing Gary's behavior was so revealing and served as a catalyst to begin my own recovery from childhood traumas. While Gary's family was more dysfunctional than my own, I knew I had unresolved issues. The key indicator of that was understanding what needs in my own programming had led me to marry him in the first place. For example, in recalling my husband's funeral, I held no memory of my father's presence. I remember Uncle Wayne being there in a loving and supportive manner. My father was physically present but emotionally unavailable. Seeking answers to "why" and "if only" questions led me to discover many unresolved losses of my own.

Life is filled with "mini" and "many" losses. Too often, professionals in the grief area do not give enough attention to accumulating "mini" losses. The addiction literature is mushrooming now with information on healing from earlier childhood traumas and losses. I took advantage of reading anything I could find that I thought would be helpful. I also filled several bound journals.

My recovery required that I get in touch with those early traumatic experiences and the feelings which accompanied those traumas. Defense mechanisms such as repression, denial, psychic numbing, and disassociation protected me at the time, but they represent survival techniques. Loss of memory of childhood experiences is a good indicator of abuse or depression. These defense mechanisms, if employed, will impede the healthy resolution of loss. This phenomenon of unresolved grief is connected to what grief experts would label as a delayed, inhibited, or chronic grief reaction. Gary had a delayed grief reaction. A description of dysfunctional families follows to clarify the connection between dysfunctional families and dysfunctional grief.

Dysfunctional Families

My usage of two descriptors needs clarification. I am often asked, "What do you mean by an adult child?" Professional colleagues in education have suggested that it sounds almost derogatory to refer to an adult as a child. Dysfunctional families have become the norm. Yet, many educators are uninformed. Part of the reason for this ignorance is that many adult children are educators or counselors. These adult children have evolved at a very high level intellectually but emotionally still carry unhealed wounds from their own childhood traumas.

Another area where some people are not well versed is what represents abuse: I recently talked about a woman who was abused. The first response of a male colleague, who was listening to my description, was, "Did he hit her? Is that what you mean by abuse?" Abuse in a dysfunctional family covers a wide range of behaviors and is experienced by family members in different ways. Physical abuse is an invasion of our privacy and physical boundaries. We have a clearer understanding of physical boundary invasion. We also readily understand that sexual abuse is another invasion of the physical boundary. However, sexual abuse is also an invasion of one's emotional and spiritual boundaries; it totally disregards the self. I did not experience sexual abuse and recall only one incident where my father kicked me because I lost my balance on the swing while I was holding Charles, and we fell off. I was confused because it was an accident, and I would never hurt my brother on purpose.

Emotional and verbal abuse is extremely destructive to one's sense of self. The wounds for both are difficult to "make real". Emotional abuse is less recognized, less understood, and more difficult to overcome. Emotional invasion can be really devastating and virtually leave the child without a sense of protective boundaries. Emotional incest occurs when an adult shares intimate, painful information about the other parent with a child. This emotional intimacy invasion is also referred to as enmeshment. Because the child does not possess the developmental skills nor the power to address the problem, the experience is emotionally traumatizing. Depending upon the level of dysfunction in the family, multiple boundary invasions may occur. I felt like I was the space between my mother and father. My primary responsibility was to entertain Dad and keep him happy. This was an impossible task sometimes.

I discovered a very insightful book called *Adult Children: Secrets of Dysfunctional Families* by John and Linda Friel. They proposed a model which allowed me to understand that dysfunctional families occur for many reasons and not merely because of drug addiction. A family can become dysfunctional if any compulsive behavior is present, mental illness, rigid rules, religiosity, and any situation where the outer circumstances seek to control rather than facilitate the emergence of a strong inner sense of self, personal power, and life skill competency development. I learned that dysfunctional family patterns continue to re-emerge in different forms in the second and third generations unless recovery is accomplished. The family does not suddenly become healthy when the drinking or compulsive behavior stops.

I learned that dysfunctional families are universal. Addiction treatment professionals suggest that 80-95 percent of families are dysfunctional to some degree. If the norm is dysfunctional, then what attributes describe a functional family? A functional family provides children with a safe and nurturing environment, supports learning during the different developmental stages, affirms the child's worth, and nurtures a sense of self-confidence and autonomy. If the addiction treatment community is correct, most people reading this chapter have experienced some wounding that may need healing. The life experiences that caused those wounds will most likely be included in the life review when a family member who caused, or failed to protect a child from harm, dies. My response to my second husband's grief and research into dysfunctional families led me to begin my own recovery. It helped me tremendously because my parents were elderly and ill. I began an "anticipatory grief" reaction with the deliberate intent to finish my unfinished business with them before they died. Both parents are now deceased. I knew exactly when my father passed from a heart attack. I was in a meeting of community people discussing debriefing after the tornado that hit our town when I got the call. I raced to my car to head home and then sensed Daddy's presence. I stopped the car and simply said out loud, "Go easy, Daddy. Be at peace."

When our mother died of breast cancer, she was in a coma when I told her goodbye. I traveled to Alabama for a deposition I was scheduled to give for attorneys in a "wrongful" cremation lawsuit. I asked for a break to call home and learned from Uncle Wayne that Mom had passed peacefully. I struggled with guilt about not being there with her. Weeks later, my sister-in-law called me to say that she felt compelled to tell me that I had nothing to feel guilty about because I was doing exactly what my mother would have wanted...helping someone else. I firmly believe that souls can communicate with people. This belief is based on my own experience and what I have heard from many others. For example, Chris and I were the last family members to see Mama Keith before she died. I was sleeping on a friend's couch in Morehead when Mama's presence awakened me. I felt her love and sensed her apology for allowing her older sons to treat me the way they had. I did not see her, nor did I hear her words. I sensed and felt them.

Those who grew up in a dysfunctional family or were neglected or abused in different ways are disenfranchised in our childhood grief. Our losses in childhood have not been honored; they have been disregarded. As children from dysfunctional families, we have disowned our true selves; we did so to survive. Let me add that I love both my parents and recognize that they were better parents than their mothers and fathers. Part of the recovery process of this disenfranchised grief also includes forgiveness and making peace with one's parents. When I began my recovery work, I did not feel comfortable being with my parents. It was too easy to slip back into the use of the defense mechanisms and to become caught up in the roles and messages. Later as I became stronger, being with my family was helpful. Therefore, I could remain detached and observe their behavior and my responses more realistically. As in the numbing and denial phases of grief, children of trauma also have difficulty making their losses real. Support groups where persons can validate your experiences are helpful, or the loss may never be resolved.

Roles in the Dysfunctional Family

Imagine a child's mobile. Each element in the mobile represents a family role. Roles are played out subconsciously to keep the family on an even keel. Roles may be exchanged, and different family members may play more than one role. The person plays the first role with the principal dysfunction. That person's behavior is out-of-control. The role of the enabler balances the addict. The enabler gradually assumes greater responsibility for the family and attempts to control the behavior of the addict. As the addict loses control over their behavior, the enabler attempts to regain control and balance. Both are preoccupied with this interactive dance. If these two persons represent parents in a family system, one can easily understand the lack of appropriate nurturing and role modeling for children.

Another role played in the family system, which is intended to maintain balance, is the hero child. The hero child looks really good, tries to be perfect, makes straight A's, maybe captain of the football team, attends school regularly, participates in many school functions, and then comes home to help take care of the other children. The hero assumes a great deal of family responsibility when the sick person starts acting out. The enabler tries to control the craziness, and both parents abandon the children. Abandonment is a common issue in dysfunctional families. The hero child abandons their childhood; the parents abandon the children; the addict abandons the spouse. Therefore, loss is a frequent occurrence in dysfunctional families. Death represents the ultimate abandonment.

The hero tries to pick up the slack of both parents. The hero is the family member who tries to excel in life. They may become a doctor, therapist, teacher, etc. Heroes are extremely responsible and productive. However, they are failures in the area where they contribute the most energy. They fail to protect the family from pain. The addiction literature suggests that hero children are likely to commit suicide to escape this realization.

To balance this family mobile, however, someone has to be responsible for all the family pain. The scapegoat role is represented by the child who wrecks the car, gets pregnant, gets someone else pregnant, gets into fights, steals, abuses drugs, etc. Their behavior is negative. The scapegoat is frequently told that the family would be okay if they were more like the hero. When a death occurs, the scapegoat is often not a guest at the funeral. Much anger and resentment are projected upon this individual prior to the death and during the mourning period.

The next role is the mascot. The mascot is the child who tries to bring humor and joy to the family. The mascot plans parties, buys presents, and is generally a good stand-up comic. When the pain becomes too intense, the mascot tries to find a way to make the family laugh.

The final role played in the dysfunctional family is the lost child. If you tried to visualize all the people in your high school class, lost children are those whose names you cannot remember. They make average grades, are quiet, and try to fade into the wall. The lost child is trying to avoid pain. The lost child obviously wants to escape. Running away or taking "long-distance" cures by moving hundreds of miles from family are two strategies often employed. The lost child is most likely to commit suicide. The lost child is also the least likely to attend the funeral.

Each family member becomes disassociated from their real self. Everyone becomes a reactor. Thus, co-dependency emerges. Control is a major issue for anyone who grows up in a dysfunctional family. Each person needs to be in control and wants desperately to keep the peace.

By comparing the traits of the authentic self to the co-dependent self and considering negative messages/negative rules in these families, we can begin to understand the belief system that creates so much conflict for bereaved persons.

These lists of descriptors are taken from Dr. Charles Whitfield's book *Healing the Child Within* [1, p.10].

Real Self

* authentic
* true self
* genuine
* spontaneous
* expansive
* loving
* giving
* communicating
* accepting of self and others
* compassionate
* love unconditionally
* feels feelings, including appropriate and spontaneous current anger
* assertive
* intuitive
* honors the inner child
* natural child plays and has fun
* vulnerable

* powerful

* trusting

* enjoys being nurtured

* surrenders

* self-indulgent

* open to the unconscious

* remembers our oneness

* free to grow

* private self

Co-dependent Self

* alienated from self

* unauthentic

* false

* not genuine

* acts "as if" personality

* plans and plots

* contracting

* fearful

* withholding

* envious

* critical

* idealized

* perfectionistic

* other-oriented
* overly conforming
* loves conditionally
* denies or hides feelings, including long-held anger and resentment
* aggressive or passive/aggressive
* is rational and logical rather than intuitive
* overdeveloped adult scripts
* super responsible people who avoid playing and having fun
* pretend always to be strong
* limited personal power
* distrusting
* avoids being nurtured
* lacks self-control
* withdraws
* self-righteous
* blocks some conscious material
* forgets our oneness
* feels separate
* tends to repeat painful patterns unconsciously, especially in marriages like those modeled by parents

* public self

Negative rules and negative messages complete the belief system in a dysfunctional family. If you want a more in-depth analysis of your own belief system, consult C. Steiner's Scripts People Live [2]. You can probably get some idea of your family scripts by paying attention to those statements that "trigger" you as you read the following list.

Universal rules in a family system are don't talk, don't trust, and don't feel. The need for rules is pretty obvious. You don't talk about the real problem; your parents are unreliable, so you cannot trust them; there is a lot of pain in the family which no one will recognize, so feelings are unimportant; don't express your feelings; don't get angry; don't get upset; don't cry; do as I say not as I do; be good; be nice; be perfect; avoid conflict or avoid dealing with conflict. Again, Dr. Whitfield (1, p. 47) gives us insights into messages from dysfunctional families.

Negative Messages

* Shame on you
* You're not good enough
* I wish I had never had you
* Your needs are not all right with me
* Hurry up and grow up

* Be dependent

* Be a man

* Always look good

* Maintain the status quo

* Everyone in the family must be an enabler

* That's not true

* I promise, then promises are broken

* Don't think or talk; just follow the rules

* Do well in school

* Don't ask any questions

* Don't betray the family

* Don't discuss the family with outsiders

* Keep the family secret

* Be seen and not heard

* No back talk

* I'm sacrificing myself for you

* You're driving me crazy

* You'll never amount to anything

* It really didn't hurt

* You're so selfish

* You'll be the death of me, yet

* Don't contradict me

* Big boys don't cry

* Don't be like that
* Act like a girl or lady
* You don't feel that way
* You're so stupid or bad
* You caused it
* You owe it to me
* Of course, we love you

The "looking good" dysfunctional family seems to be functional for all outward appearances. They wear the right clothes, say the right things, and belong to the right groups; they look perfect on the outside, but no true intimacy exists. Family members' emotional needs are not met. Again, the question of suicide emerges. We all know "good" families where a member has committed suicide, and the entire community is shocked. The family has difficulty understanding also because their view is that the family was meeting all the individual's needs.

Unifying Model

We now have a unifying model of co-dependency and compulsive behaviors described by John and Linda Friel in their book *Adult Children: Secrets of Dysfunctional Families*. The model is called an iceberg model because frozen core feelings and issues depicted below the water line are common to all children from dysfunctional families. At the very bottom, the inner core issue is a fear of abandonment. Shame and guilt are next, but there is a difference between shame and guilt. Guilt is described as a conflict in your behaviors and values. The message is, "Your behavior is inappropriate". The message reflected in shame is, "You're no good. You're bad to the core". Shame issues are identified by listening to feelings which is difficult for children of trauma. Above that is a layer identified as co-dependency and intimacy problems. Co-dependents either have difficulty attaching or act like leeches. They have no separate self; they become so obsessed and involved with another person that they don't know what they think or what they believe. They go along with whatever the other person wants, thinks, and needs. For example, co-dependents whose spouses die have more difficulty making decisions because they can no longer assess what the spouse would do. Those co-dependents quickly transfer their dependency to children or another adult.

This model depicts a projection above the water line of resulting problems in many different forms: compulsive behaviors that include chemical addiction, eating disorders, relationship addictions; stress disorders; depression; compulsions.

I propose adding another layer in the frozen feelings

area, directly above guilt. That layer would be entitled "unresolved grief from losses". The recovery process for adult children parallels Dr. William Worden's four tasks of mourning; accepting reality; being with the feelings; adjusting roles and responsibilities, and renewing life. In the addiction literature, the first stage is emerging awareness which includes an understanding that what happened in the family was not okay. The person begins to "make real" the pain that was felt. Reading helps remove the layers of denial. I encourage journaling and reading to assist the person in staying in touch with feelings and associated events. Dreams are also important at this time. I also find it helpful to "highlight" a book that is particularly meaningful because subsequent readings will reveal even more important insights. Because of repression, denial, and psychic numbing, the person's psyche is protected from revealing too much information quickly. If this does occur, "flooding" and "flashbacks" will result. The person may shut down altogether as a survival strategy. The individual is encouraged to conduct the life review slowly during this time. The second stage is identifying core issues such as the need to control, fear of intimacy, neglecting needs, etc. The third stage is transformation. Integration occurs when the individual begins to change the way they respond. Giant steps in personal growth are taken during the transformation and integration stages.

Again, the addiction literature helps summarize how healing occurs. According to Charles Whitfield, the first step for an adult child is to discover and practice being his real self. Many people recovering from a death find that they become more centered, whole, and aligned with their true selves.

The second step is identifying our ongoing physical, mental, emotional, and spiritual needs and practicing getting these needs with safe and supportive people. A safe person will listen, accept your feelings, honor your feelings, not discount or invalidate feelings, honor your confidence, and not attempt to tell you what to do. These are few and far between in the grieving person's world. These safe people empower you to believe in yourself. They do not betray you.

Thirdly, Dr. Whitfield suggests we must identify, re-experience, and grieve the pain of our losses and traumas in the presence of safe and supportive people. The fourth step is to identify and work through our core issues and be responsible for our own recovery. It is amazing how closely these steps parallel grief recovery. There is much that grief counselors and death educators can learn from the adult children's recovery movement. More research is needed regarding suicide and how it correlates to dysfunctional family rules, messages, and roles. It is quite possible that studies in the dysfunctional family area will provide the key to facilitating the resolution of dysfunctional or pathological grief. I strongly believe that many of the "complicated" mourning cases that are so difficult for therapists to assist the client with are rooted in unresolved dysfunctional family issues.

Ambiguous Loss is a new concept presented by Dr. Pauline Boss in her book *Loss, Trauma, and Resilience.* The concept emerged from clinical work with victims of the Oklahoma City Bombing, 911, and the tsunami, where bodies were never found. The concept also includes such losses as family members with dementia or Alzheimer's disease, mental illness, AIDS/HIV, drug abuse, and grandparents who are separated from their grandchildren due to family conflict. Children are profoundly affected by such losses because there is no opportunity for closure and the loss is chronic and ongoing. Dysfunctional family systems that enforce the "don't talk" rule is prone to experience ambiguous loss. Family counseling is highly recommended to provide the family system with support to openly communicate about the change in circumstances, the need to hold onto hope, redefine boundaries, and establish new family rituals.

Chapter Eight: Journal Your Losses and Traumas

Getting started on any writing project is challenging. First of all, remember that everything you have lived through, you have already survived. You are going back in your memory to clean up any leftover issues. Second, no one but you is going to read your journal unless you give them permission to do so. Third, your writing skills are not important. This process allows you to cleanse yourself of old painful experiences that still negatively impact your life.

Read each journal entry prompt that I have given you, think about the questions, and then write. If a prompt does not bring anything to mind, move to the next one, but discipline yourself not to avoid writing about anything you have been suppressing or avoiding. Do it because you are worth it!

Journal Entry: Describe your parents' upbringing. How were they disciplined? How did they show emotions? How did they communicate? Was there any dysfunction in their parents' family systems?

Journal Entry: How was death handled in your parents' families? Describe your parents' reactions and the services you attended. How old were you when your grandparents died? Did you attend their funeral services? How did you feel?

Journal Entry: Make a list of all losses and traumas you can remember and the age you were when they occurred. Describe them one at a time, including how you felt, what you thought, what other people did, and what was the worst part for you.

Journal Entry: Does anyone in your biological family system have any dysfunctional patterns? Look for any past patterns in your relationships with your parents or significant people and describe them. Do you have any dysfunctional patterns that are carryovers from your family system? What was your assigned role in the family?

Journal Entry: Describe how you came to meet the person or persons you are grieving now.

Journal Entry: The person who died is special. Introduce this individual by describing their life beginning as far back as you can remember. If you have multiple losses to process, repeat this description for each.

Journal Entry: Continue by writing about what you remember as most important to you in your relationship with this person at the beginning of your lives together. Describe your relationship with this person.

Journal Entry: What were the special traits of your loved one?

Journal Entry: Write about where you were and how you learned about the death or terminal illness. Include your thoughts, feelings, and physical responses to the news. Also, write about what other people did or said that upset you. The first task of mourning is accepting the reality of the death. Depending on the circumstances of the death, that task may be more difficult for some people.

Journal Entry: Describe your loved one's death.

Journal Entry: If your loved one had a lengthy illness or emergency treatment at a hospital, hospice or accident scene, there could be many unfinished issues related to their care. Describe the experience that stands out as significant or still troubling you. Include the people, professionals, and family and friends, who shared this experience with you. Describe both positive and negative experiences.

Journal Entry: If you were with your loved one when they passed, describe what happened. Include what you did after the death was confirmed.

Journal Entry: In my family growing up, death was viewed as…

Journal Entry: What does death mean to you? Describe your thoughts, feelings, and spiritual beliefs.

Journal Entry: When someone died, my parents…

Journal Entry: My earliest memory of death was…

Journal Entry: The most difficult death I experienced as a child was…

Funerals can be so painful that they leave you feeling like a dark cloud is hanging over you. If that was your experience, you might not remember much about who was there or what was said. Some people hold onto negative memories about the funeral because they have so little time to discuss the positive and negative things that happened. Think about how your loved one's visitation, funeral, graveside, memorial service or celebration of life was handled. Write about these services.

Journal Entry: Do you have any regrets? Are there some things that you want to remember?

Journal Entry: It is quite normal to think about things that might have happened differently after a death has occurred. You may ask "why," "what if," or "if only" questions. Regardless of the possibilities, you may consider, nothing can change the reality now. That is what you are really searching for… a way to change what happened. Write about your questions and answers.

Journal Entry: If I had one more opportunity to talk with the deceased, I would say…

Journal Entry: Focus your attention on accepting what you cannot change, and think about what lesson you learned that would guide how you live your life in the future. Write about that new awareness and commitment.

Journal Entry: Describe your own experience with hope and despair. In our life review following a loss, we often focus on every little thing we regret rather than all the things we feel very positive about. To be human is to be imperfect. Today if you remember something that happened that you regret, you can forgive yourself rather than dwell on it. Then deliberately focus on something you did which you feel good about. Affirm yourself for releasing regrets and reminding yourself of previous good deeds. Write about these affirmations and regrets.

Journal Entry: I regret...

Journal Entry: I wish I had…

Journal Entry: I wish I had not…

Journal Entry: If I could live my life over, I would…

Journal Entry: I am imperfect, but parts of me are excellent. My strengths are…

Journal Entry: If I had one more opportunity to talk with the deceased, I would say…

Journal Entry: The things I miss most are…

Journal Entry: The things I enjoyed most were…

Journal Entry: Describe how you used food and drink before and after the death.

If eating habits have changed, resulting in loss or excessive weight gain, this is an indication that you may need to see your physician and be evaluated for depression.

Journal Entry: Are you using drugs and alcohol to cope? What, how much, and how often do you use? Do you think you need help quitting?

Journal Entry: Taking care of me and my life is… hard, difficult, easy… Describe how your life changed after the death.

Journal Entry: The most challenging time of the day is…

Journal Entry: I feel most alone when…

Journal Entry: Write about what you resent.

Journal Entry: Social isolation can become a problem when grieving because you make people around you uncomfortable with their inadequacies or fears. Whose support have you lost from your friends or family? Write about these uncomfortable experiences.

Journal Entry: Describe how your sleep patterns changed. If you have difficulty falling asleep, staying asleep, or waking early in the morning and are unable to fall back asleep. In that case, this indicates that you may need to see your physician and be evaluated for depression. Similarly, if you want to sleep all the time to escape the pain, you need to talk to your physician.

Journal Entry: Who can you count on to be there for you? Who did you lose as friends after the death?

Journal Entry: I worry about…

Journal Entry: To address these worries, the actions I can take are…

Journal Entry: Sometimes, it is helpful to make lists to sort out what you are thinking.

Today focus on one problem you can solve. What action will you take to resolve that problem?

Journal Entry: Recognizing safe people who are comfortable letting you talk about your loved one is sometimes tricky. Think about your family and friends. With whom do you feel safe talking about your feelings and concerns? The traits of a safe person are: being a good listener, not giving advice, keeping what you share confidential, being there when you need them either in person or on the phone, never reflecting a sense of incompetency on your part, and reminding you of your strengths.

Journal Entry: Who are your unsafe people? What have they done that tells you they are unsafe? Describe what these individuals did that makes you uncomfortable and feel unsafe.

Journal Entry: The greatest fear I have is…

Journal Entry: People say things sometimes without thinking. Their comments can be insensitive. Describe how others have treated you inappropriately or said "dumb and stupid" things. How can you put aside this insensitivity which is often due to a lack of awareness? What are some of the cliches people said to you? How did you feel when you heard those cliches'?

Journal Entry: What are some of the issues you struggle to resolve in your wall of pain?

Journal Entry: What are the most significant issues you have difficulty processing?

Journal Entry: The things you do that help you cope are…

Journal Entry: What are the life lessons you have learned from loss?

Journal Entry: One thing you would like to change about your life is…

Journal Entry: Your favorite memory of your loved one is… Keep coming back to this each time you identify another good memory.

Journal Entry: The ways in which your life has changed since the death are… Keep coming back to this each time you come to a new realization.

Journal Entry: Sometimes, we focus only on the positive aspects of our loved ones. We are all human, including your loved one. Your loved one's weaknesses were…

Journal Entry: Your loved one's strengths were…

Journal Entry: Your loved one taught you…

Journal Entry: It is difficult accepting the death of a loved one. Reaching a point of acceptance that they are dead may take weeks or even months. Think about your own experiences of denial, fantasy, avoidance, etc. and write about them. The first task of mourning is accepting death is final. Describe your progress with each task: acceptance of the death, life review and resolution of conflicts, adjusting roles and responsibilities, and renewing life.

Journal Entry: Making decisions alone can sometimes be difficult, especially if you were accustomed to discussing them with your loved one. What decision are you struggling with today?

Journal Entry: Who among your safe family and friends is best suited to be a sounding board without giving you advice?

Consider this affirmation: While I may seek out others to serve as objective listeners, I trust myself now to make the best decision. It is helpful sometimes to have others serve as a sounding board for our problems. However, becoming too dependent upon others in decision-making robs us of the opportunity to honor our own personal power and to improve our decision-making skills. To regain confidence in ourselves, we can grow through taking risks, making our own decisions and accepting that we can also cope with whatever consequences.

Journal Entry: Write about any mistakes you feel you have made. Describe why you think you made a mistake. Then write about your decisions that led to positive outcomes.

Journal Entry: What troubles you most about the death or your relationship with the deceased?

Journal Entry: Stressed out! There are days when you feel like you can't take it anymore! If one more thing happens, you will scream or did scream. Write about what happened and your feelings.

Journal Entry: What problems have you had to deal with that you would just as soon live without?

Journal Entry: Going out alone? Why is it difficult? What can you do to relieve this distress? Who can you invite to accompany you? What uncomfortable thoughts and feelings do you experience when you think about going out alone? Is there a specific place that holds important memories for you that will be hard to visit? For example, the place where the death occurred can be either "sacred" ground or filled with great pain.

Journal Entry: Is there an issue you have been avoiding? Are there things that you, the deceased, or other people do that causes you constant pain? Write about those events or issues. Are you willing to forgive? What barriers block you from forgiving? Forgiving does not mean you approve of wrongdoing. It does mean you want to release the anger associated with the wrongdoing or the desire to punish.

Journal Entry: Do you have unresolved issues with the deceased where you need to apologize and ask forgiveness? If so, write the deceased a letter addressing your feelings, expressing regret, and ask for forgiveness. Read the letter aloud and then visualize your loved one forgiving you.

Journal Entry: What or who is essential in your life before the death? What or who was influential in the life of the deceased? Our values become clear as we grieve. What or who is important to you now? We become less tolerant of petty behaviors and self-indulged people. Frankly, I developed zero tolerance for bullshit and drama queens.

Journal Entry: We can all grow from loss. It is important sometimes to reflect upon how we have become more robust. By looking retrospectively at our lives, we can see growth that may not be clearly visible on a daily basis. You have survived, to date, the worst thing that could have happened to you. You are slowly putting your life back together. How have you grown from your personal life experiences?

Journal Entry: You can achieve everything in your life that you choose. To achieve great things, you must be willing to dream. Sit quietly and think about what positive things you want in your life. Imagine these things are already present, and be aware of your feelings. Your thoughts and feelings are my reality. You can choose to have thoughts and feelings that are positive and nurturing for you today.

Journal Entry: What do you want your life to include in the future? What is your dream for the future that you would like to make come true? New opportunities will be available to you each day if you allow yourself to take risks. Taking risks means that you exercise your right to choose your life experiences.

Journal Entry: What choices can you make today that will open the door to new opportunities? What goals can you set for yourself? What steps can you take today toward achieving a goal?

Journal Entry: Finding joy again is possible, and you find it through small experiences like the smell of coffee or a flower, the sweet antics of a child, a sunset, listening to the rain, etc.

Develop a "Bliss List" of small experiences that bring you pleasure. Recognize that it is tough to find things you enjoy while grieving. Usually, small rays of light appear through the shadows of your grief… to remind you how to feel joy again. My list was simple, my children, flowers, birds, butterflies, coffee in the morning, and friends.

Journal Entry: Some of us never learned how to nurture ourselves, and those that do often stop taking care of themselves. How do you nurture yourself? If you find that you seldom do anything to nurture yourself, make a list of little things that you could do to take better care of yourself.

Journal Entry: What are the questions for which you may never find answers? What are the issues that may never be resolved? Which of these are you ready to accept?

Journal Entry: What bothers you the most now?

Journal Entry: Are there times when you focus your thoughts on things you think you "should" do? What "should" thoughts do you need to release?

Journal Entry: When you allow others to invade your personal space emotionally, physically, or spiritually, you are also allowing them to take away your personal power. Sometimes well-meaning friends or family will take charge of tasks or responsibilities without asking. Who takes away your personal power? What limits can you set for that person today?

Journal Entry: What memories bring you joy? Recalling them may be bittersweet at first because you long for the deceased. As you gradually accept the death, the longing will decline in intensity, and the joy associated with the memory will become stronger. What memories are associated with joy?

Journal Entry: Life is today… the past is gone… what can you do to make today meaningful?

Journal Entry: Your favorite memory of your loved one is...

Journal Entry: Unfinished business needs to be processed and released. If you have something positive, you wish you had said to your loved one, write the person a letter expressing your feelings.

Journal Entry: Special days – Difficult days. Some days are more difficult than others... anniversaries, birthdays... which days will be most difficult for you and why? What can you do to prepare for that day so that you can not only cope but also celebrate the life of your loved one? Plan what you will do in advance. Discuss it with family members who may be affected. Encourage them to do something special too.

Journal Entry: In our grief, we often have issues that represent our greatest pain. They are "tender spots" that are with us for life. What is the cause of your greatest pain? For a long time, I had difficulty being with and seeing couples together. Describe your "tender spots."

Journal Entry: A certain amount of alone time is necessary for you to heal. However, we can isolate ourselves from people who are supportive and who can help us find balance again in our lives. Have you withdrawn from people? Why? What can you do to overcome this?

Journal Entry: What social, recreational, or community service activities would you like to do to help others? Sometimes it is easier to involve ourselves in something meaningful rather than activities that merely distract us, such as sports or recreational activities. Are there community service projects that could be done in memory of your loved one? Write about those that interest you.

Journal Entry: How has your life changed since the death? Describe the negative changes first. Then describe the positive changes or how you have compensated for the negative changes.

Journal Entry: If you do not care for yourself, who will? We often feel insecure and needy after a significant loss. You can meet all your own needs if you accept the responsibility instead of looking to others to lean on or to protect you. What can you do today to take better care of yourself?

Journal Entry: For years, our lives can stay focused on achievements. Owning a home, earning a degree, making a specific salary, etc., are important goals. However, some people find after achieving goals that, unhappiness still prevails. Happiness is a state of being and cannot be achieved in the future. It can only be experienced in the present moment. Happiness resides within us through our experiences of positive feelings with those we love… or conflicts in our beliefs and experiences with our loved ones keep us distressed and block positive feelings and experiences in the present. You can commit to either staying stuck in the negative or choose to be open to the good and positive experiences in the present. What do you choose for yourself?

Journal Entry: What attributes are unique to you? After the death of someone special, we often lose our sense of worth because that individual affirmed us. Learning to value and honor ourselves is crucial in our recovery. We can do this by affirming ourselves. You can be reminded of your strengths by making positive statements to yourself. You can also build your inner strength and confidence. What can you do well? Write about your strengths and try not to use diminishing qualifying statements, such as "I am pretty good." Instead, say, "I am good."

Sometimes we can become bogged down in anxiety over what might happen. Feeling anxious after a loss is normal, but we must learn to address the underlying causes. When you feel anxious, you can be quiet with your feelings and determine the source of your anxiety. When you understand what you feel, you can begin to take positive steps to overcome these feelings. You can remind yourself that no one is perfect. You have already survived the worst thing that could happen to you– the death of a loved one. Whatever happens today, you can handle it.

You must release your pain. Holding onto it accomplishes nothing positive. Being in pain is not a measure of your love for the deceased. Initially, your pain may have been about your loved one's suffering or longing for their presence. Your pain may also be a measure of your regrets about your behaviors as you experienced life with the deceased. A true measure of your love for the deceased is to be able to experience the positive things you shared and allow those memories to fill you up with joy. How has your focus on memories changed?

Journal Entry: What leftover pain from the past do you need to release today?

Journal Entry: How can I nurture myself with positive memories?

In what area of your life do you still feel insecure? Have you felt this way before in your life? How old were you when you felt that way? Remind yourself that you are an adult capable of caring for your problems and needs. You will feel more secure when you have taken steps to solve problems.

Journal Entry: What can you do to relieve your insecure feelings?

Journal Entry: How can you affirm your strengths?

It is possible to experience personal growth following a loss if you are introspective and seek insight into life's meaning. These insights generally come from experiencing emotional pain and seeking to understand it.

Journal Entry: In what areas of your life today can you choose to experience new awareness and personal growth? Sometimes we spend our time focused externally on others or others' expectations. It is easy when we are in pain to focus outward away from the pain. However, if we focus on others too much, we fail to honor our pain, learn our life lessons, and direct our lives in the areas that are important to us, not others. Where is your focus now?

Journal Entry: What or who do you value in your life today? How can you spend your time more constructively on the tasks or experiences that are truly important to you?

Regrets over past decisions and behaviors can eat away at our positive feelings. Regrets can show us where our behavior conflicts with what we value. Understanding these conflicts can help us to clarify what is truly important to us and help us make better choices in the future.

Journal Entry: What choices have you made that you wish you had handled differently? Can you do anything to correct that situation now?

Journal Entry: In what areas of your life do you feel insecure or hold onto negative beliefs that you would like to turn into a positive belief or situation? You can grow and change. To begin this process, identify your areas of insecurity and negative beliefs. Then write an affirmation statement reflecting a positive belief to fit each area you would like to change. For example, "I would like to change (or get a) job, but I am insecure about what I can do." Affirmation: I am capable of learning new things.

Switching your thoughts from a painful experience to a more positive one requires you deliberately change your thoughts. Practice telling yourself to stop and think of something else. Visualize your loved one in a beautiful, serene place filled with warm light and unconditional love. Do this several times a day for a week. Write about how you feel. Then visualize yourself experiencing that same kind of love. Know that you have God's presence and love with you always. It comes from within you. You, too, can give unconditional love.

Journal Entry: Who can you practice loving unconditionally now?

We must let go of our pain to create space within us for joy. What painful event can you release today? After you release this pain, visualize yourself feeling lighter. Releasing

pain is an active process that produces something positive...
more energy for living.

Journal Entry: Thanksgiving is a day to share and experience gratitude for our opportunities. It is a time to remember the good times shared with those who are no longer with us. It is also a time to create new memories with those we cherish who are still a living part of our lives. This Thanksgiving, you can remember happy memories from the past with gratitude, and you can also take the opportunity to create new joyful experiences. You have many reasons for being thankful. Special people share life experiences with you. Make a list of what you are grateful for in the past and now. How can you show your love and appreciation for individuals in your life today?

Journal Entry: Christmas is a special family event, filled with many rituals that bring individuals together in a joyful celebration. When a family member dies, all the rituals will be affected. Other members of the family will have to assume the roles left vacant by the death of a loved one. While the holiday will be different regardless of how these roles and rituals are fulfilled, this day does not have to be filled with sadness. Expecting to experience some pain due to reminders of the deceased is normal. Expecting to experience some joy and planning for joyful interchanges among living family members is like buying insurance. Happiness can be shared if we choose to create it. What can you do for yourself and your family to make the Christmas holiday a joyful experience?

Anniversary Reactions: The first anniversary of the death is especially hard. When you begin reliving the death's circumstances, you begin to experience the anniversary. This may happen about 6 weeks before the actual death date. You will return in memory to the events that transpired around the time of the death. It will feel almost as painful as it did then. If you experienced a traumatic death, you might actually feel worse than when the death occurred because you do not have shock and numbness to protect you. What can you do to focus on the positive aspects of your loved one's life? What can you plan to do on that day to celebrate them? With whom do you need to discuss these plans?

Journal Entry: What issues seem most painful now? Write about them. Avoiding thinking about them does not reduce their intensity. Facing them, head-on does. Then focus your attention on what you could do to remember the deceased in a positive way to celebrate their life. Develop a plan that feels right to you. Discuss your ideas with your family and encourage them to do something positive.

Now would be a good time to review your journal and repeat any writing activities that trigger your emotions or thoughts.

Journal Entry: Where are you going with your life? What do you want the next page of your life story to say? What do you need to do to make that happen?

Journal Entry: What decisions can you make today without needing someone else to help you? Ask yourself what is different about you. What new skills have you acquired? Where do you want to "grow" next? Instead of looking at another year with dread, understand that your healing process will continue. You are moving toward peace and joy again.

Journal Entry: What do you want to accomplish with your life in the coming year?

Journal Entry: To rely on major events and accomplishments to bring joy to your life is to rob yourself of a multitude of small pleasures. What small joyful pleasures can you experience today? For example, "I like the taste of bread pudding."

Journal Entry: You do not need to worry about a future event. If something does concern you about the future, the best you can do is to plan how you might cope with those events.

Journal Entry: What occasion or encounter do you need to pre-plan a response for today? When you have thought about how you will manage this situation, you can let go of worry, for you have done the best you can under the present circumstances.

Journal Entry: Sit quietly and reflect on what beautiful things or people you have in your life today.

Journal Entry: What or who do you still have in your life that brings you joy?

Journal Entry: What brings you peace? What do you have in your life now and in the past that you are grateful for today? Begin each day with a prayer of gratitude for what or who you have.

You may feel a stronger bond with your loved ones, including the deceased. Know that love never dies. You have the capacity to love many people. Are you ready to love new people who may come into your life? What special qualities in people will you look for in new relationships?

Epilogue

Where are all the Keith family members now? Chris grew up to be so much like his dad, Joe. He is mechanically inclined and is a fantastic father, husband, employee, friend, and son. Chris and Lynette live in northern Kentucky and have been married for 19 years. Chris finished his master's degree at the University of Cincinnati, and Lynette also finished her degree in Health Information Systems at the same University. Chris is a computer network engineer, and Lynette does medical coding for Cincinnati Children's Hospital. They have four totally awesome sons. Devon is 26, in the Air Force special forces, and married to Savannah. Dawson is 17, works part-time, does well in school, is considering colleges, and plays saxophone in the high school band and jazz band. Jackson is 16, works part-time, is doing well in school and looking forward to following in Dawson's footsteps by getting his own vehicle and learning to drive. Cohen, who is 10, is doing well in school and plays a lot! The grandsons are the joy of my life, and I make sure they know it!

As for me, four years ago, I sold my house in Berea, Kentucky, and contracted to have a retirement/vacation cottage built on Joe's Mountain. I bought a small chainsaw and cut those damned trees down before the cottage was built on the spot where Joe died. Chris was not happy with my taking that risk with the chainsaw, so I did not tell him until the deed was done. I felt it was something I needed to do. The cottage is a perfect living space for me, has room for visitors, and the upstairs loft is designated as the Grands' Cave. I occasionally offer workshops, garden, sew, read, walk with friends, sit on the deck and watch birds, butterflies, squirrels, and deer who live here with me. I am ageing as gracefully as I can at 75 full years of living through hell and back. I have fulfilled my life's purpose through my work with school staff. I am at peace and hope that this book benefits those who choose to use it in their recovery work. May you be blessed and find peace and joy again. Judy Keith, Ed.D.

References

C. Whitfield. *Healing the Child Within: Discovery and Recovery for Adult Children of*

Dysfunctional Families, Health Communications, Deerfield Beach, Florida, 1987.

C. Steiner. *Scripts People Live: Transactional Analysis of Life.* Grove Press, New York, 1974.

J. Fried and L. Friel, *Adult Children: Secrets of Dysfunctional Families,* Health Communications, Deerfield Beach, Florida, 1988.

J. Morgan, Editor. *Personal Care in an Impersonal World: A multidimensional look at Bereavement, 1993. "Growing Beyond Survival: Grief Experiences of Children From Dysfunctional Families," p.179-188.*

J.W. Worden, *Grief Counseling and Grief Therapy: A Handbook for the Mental Health Practitioner.* Springer: New York, 1982.

P. Boss, *Loss, Trauma, and Resilence: Therapeutic work with Ambiguous Loss.* W. W. Norton & Company: New York, 2006.

Books Recommended for reading by Adult Children who want to pursue recovery from growing up in a dysfunctional family:

C. Whitfield. *Healing the Child Within: Discovery and Recovery for Adult Children of Dysfunctional Families.*

D. Briggs. *Celebrate Your Self*

J. Bradshaw, *Healing the Shame That Binds You.*

J. Friel and L. Friel. *Adult Children: Secrets of Dysfunctional Families.*

J. Middleton-Moz, *Children of Trauma: Rediscovering Your Discarded Self*

J. Woltitz. *The Complete ACOA Sourcebook: Adult Children of Alcoholics at Home, at Work, and in Love*

M. Beattie. *Codependent No More: How to Stop Controlling Others and Start Caring for Yourself.*

W. Kritsberg. *The Adult Children of Alcoholics Syndrome: A Step By Step Guide to Discovery and Recovery.*

W. and Weiss, *Recovery from Co-Dependency: It's Never too Late to Reclaim Your Childhood.*

And anything else that appeals to you.

Made in the USA
Coppell, TX
21 May 2024

32592879R00075